CHILD DEVELOPMENT

(In 3 Volumes)

Children and the Media

(Volume-3)

Editor

Dr. Sujata Mittal

ISHA BOOKS

DELHI-110 033

Children and the Media

Rs. 2500 (Set)
Rs. 835 (each volume)

ISBN: 81-8205-085-5 (Set)
ISBN: 81-8205-088-X (Vol. 3)

Published in 2004 in India by
Isha Books, D-43, Prithviraj Road,
Adarsh Nagar, Delhi-110 033

Laser Typesetting at : Shree Vaishnavi Creations, Delhi
Printed at : Chawla Offset Press, Delhi

Contents

Preface

The world is flooded by the media. It has become a powerful force in children's lives. Children nowadays have wide choices: many local, national and even international radio programmes; several local television channels, hundreds of video films, many different newspapers, magazines, and even computer games and worldwide information and entertainment on the internet.

Media have positive effects on teaching and learning. They are the symbol systems that teachers and students use to represent knowledge; technologies are the tools that allow them to share their knowledge representations with others. Besides these applications the influence of media countless studies have shown that a steady diet of television, movie, music, video game, and Internet violence plays a significant role in the disheartening number of violent acts committed by youth.

This book explains how media can contribute to the development of child. The applications and challenges of media in child's life are narrated elaborately. It will serve as a valuable reference tool for all related to childcare and child development.

Editor

1

Children and the Media

The world is flooded by the media. Children nowadays have wide choices: many local, national and even international radio programmes; several local television channels, hundreds of video films, many different newspapers, magazines, and even computer games and world-wide information and entertainment on the internet. We need to accept the media, especially television, are a powerful force in children's lives.

Impacts of Media on Children

Over the last few decades, media studies and research have attempted to ascertain the effects of the media in general on the behaviour and attitudes of children and determine the longer term results of their exposure to certain types of television and video programmes in particular. The majority of empirical studies have focused on the effects of watching dramatic violence on TV and film. Numerous experimental studies, many static observational studies, and a few longitudinal studies all indicate that exposure to dramatic violence on TV and in the movies is related to violent behavior. Furthermore, a substantial body of psychological theory has developed explaining the processes through which exposure to violence in the mass media could cause both short- and long-term increases in a child's aggressive and violent behavior.

Long-term effects with children are now generally believed to be primarily due to long-term observational learning of cognitions (schemas, beliefs, and biases) supporting aggression, whereas short-term effects with adults and children are recognized as also due to priming, excitation transfer, or imitation of specific behaviors.

Most researchers of aggression agree that severe aggressive and violent behavior seldom occurs unless there is a convergence of multiple predisposing and precipitating factors such as neurophysiological abnormalities, poor child rearing, socioeconomic deprivation, poor peer relations, attitudes and beliefs supporting aggression, drug and alcohol abuse, frustration and provocation, and other factors. The evidence is already substantial that exposure to media violence is one such long-term predisposing and short-term precipitating factor.

Theoretical Perspectives

In discussing the alternative theoretical perspectives that have emerged to explain the obtained relations between exposure to violence (family, community, or mass media) and subsequent aggressive behavior in the observer, it is important to distinguish between short-term effects and longer term effects. In recent theorizing, long-term relations have been ascribed mainly to acquisition through observational learning of three social-cognitive structures: schemas about a hostile world, scripts for social problem solving that focus on aggression, and normative beliefs that aggression is acceptable.

Building on the accumulating evidence that human and primate young have an innate tendency to imitate whomever they observe, these theories propose that very young children imitate almost any specific behaviors they see. Observation of specific aggressive behaviors around them increases children's likelihood of behaving in exactly that way.

Proactive-instrumental aggressive behaviors in children 2 to 4 years old generally appear spontaneously, as may hostile temper tantrums. However, the observation of specific aggressive behaviors at that age leads to the acquisition of more coordinated aggressive scripts for social problem solving and counteracts environmental forces aimed at conditioning the child out of aggression.

As the child grows older, the social scripts acquired through observation of family, peers, community, and the mass media become more complex, abstracted, and automatic in their invocation. In addition, children's socialcognitive schemas about the world around them begin to be elaborated. In particular, extensive observation of violence around them biases children's world schemas toward attributing hostility to others' actions. Such attributions in turn increase children's likelihood of behaving aggressively.

As children mature further, normative beliefs about what social behaviors are appropriate become crystallized and begin to act as filters to limit inappropriate social behavior. Children's own behaviors influence the normative beliefs that develop, but so do the children's observations of the behaviors of those around them, including those observed in the mass media.

Social-cognitive observational learning theory postulates long-term effects of exposure to violence through the influence of exposure on the development of aggressive problem-solving scripts, hostile attributional biases, and normative beliefs approving of aggression. A major alternative or complementary theory explaining longterm effects is desensitization theory. This theory is based on the empirical fact that most humans seem to have an innate negative emotional response to observing blood, gore, and violence. Increased heart rates, perspiration, and self-reports of discomfort often accompany such exposure.

However, with repeated exposure to violence, this negative emotional response habituates, and the observer becomes desensitized. The presumption is that lack of a negative emotional response to observing violence also indicates a flat response to planning violence or thinking about violence. Thus, proactive-instrumental aggressive acts become easier to commit.

There are two other quite different theoretical perspectives that have attempted to explain long-term relations between exposure to violence and aggression without hypothesizing any direct effect of violence viewing on aggression. One theory is that aggressive behavior or a correlate of aggressive behavior stimulates exposure to violence and thus engenders the observed relation between them.

Observational studies of aggressive children do show that the aggressive child is likely to provoke others, who then respond aggressively to the child, creating a violent environment that the child "observes." For media violence, however, the usual assumption is that the aggressive child simply "likes" watching media violence more than other children do.

Drawing on social comparison theory, Huesmann elaborated on this theme by suggesting that aggressive children feel happier and more justified if they believe they are not alone in their aggression, and viewing media violence makes them feel happier because it convinces them that they are not alone.

The other alternative theory that has been widely discussed is best described as the "third variable" theory. A wide variety of demographic, family, and personal characteristics are known to be correlated both with TV viewing and with aggression, such as social class and IQ.

These theories suggest that the observed long-term positive relations between aggression and exposure to media violence are spurious and are derived from their joint association with one or more of these third variables.

These "third variable" explanations should not be confused with the developmental perspectives on the observational learning and desensitization theories, which also assign important roles to parenting, intellectual ability, and social class as contributors to both exposure to violence and acceptability of aggressive behavior. Children of lower socioeconomic status (SES) and lower IQ are known to watch more TV, probably for multiple reasons including social norms, cost of alternative entertainments, and frustration with more intellectually demanding tasks. Parents' TV habits and child-rearing practices also influence the child's TV habits.

Of course, early parenting factors such as harsh punishment, rejection of the child, and lack of discipline are also known to influence subsequent aggression by the child. The difference is that these factors are viewed not as explaining away the "effect" of exposure to violence on aggression but as explaining individual differences in exposure to violence and individual differences in the strength of the effect.

Any of these theoretical processes might also contribute to the shorter term relations between exposure to violence and aggressive behavior. However, two other processes have been widely discussed as playing a role in short-term relations: priming and arousal processes. The observation of stimuli that have been paired in the past with observed violence or that inherently suggest violence (e.g., weapons) activates memory traces for aggressive scripts, schemas, and beliefs sufficiently to make their utilization more probable.

A provocation that follows a priming stimulus is more likely to stimulate aggression as a result of the priming. Although this effect is short-lived, the primed script, schema, or belief may have been acquired long ago and may have been acquired in a completely different context. To the extent that observed violence (real world or media) arouses the observer, aggressive behavior may become more likely in the short run for two other possible reasons: excitation transfer and general arousal. First, a subsequent provocation may be perceived as more severe than it is because the emotional response stimulated by the observed violence is misattributed as being due to the provocation. Such excitation transfer could account for a more intense aggressive response in the short run. Alternatively, the increased general arousal stimulated by the observed violence may simply reach such a peak that the ability of inhibiting mechanisms such as normative beliefs to restrain aggression is reduced.

It is important to recognize that these theoretical processes are not mutually exclusive. It is perfectly possible both that observational learning, desensitization, priming, and excitation transfer all contribute to the stimulation of aggression by the observation of violence and that more aggressive children do like to watch more violence. However, there is one theory that is incompatible with all of these processes. Catharsis theory would predict that violence viewing should be followed by reductions in aggression. Because the empirical evidence for any such negative relation is almost nonexistent, catharsis theory seems untenable at this time.

Empirical Background

In contrived experimental studies, children (both boys and girls) exposed to violent behavior on film or TV behave more aggressively immediately afterward. The typical paradigm involves randomly selected children who are shown either a violent or nonviolent short film and are observed afterward as they play with each other. The consistent finding is that children who see the violent film clip behave more aggressively toward each other or toward surrogate objects. In these settings, exposure to violent film scenes clearly causes more aggressive behavior by children immediately afterward.

The demonstration of a relation between the observation of dramatic TV or film violence and the commission of aggressive behavior has not been limited to the laboratory. Evidence from field studies has clearly shown that the amount of TV and film violence a child is regularly watching is positively related to the child's aggressiveness. Children who watch more violence on TV and in the movies behave more violently and express beliefs more accepting of aggressive behavior. Although the correlations are modest by the standards used in the measurement of intellectual abilities, they are highly replicable and are substantial by public health standards. Moreover, the correlation between childhood exposure to media violence and childhood aggression is highly replicable even across researchers who disagree about the reasons and across countries. Although these one-shot field studies showing a correlation between media-violence viewing and aggression suggest that the causal conclusions of the experimental studies may well generalize to the real world, longitudinal studies with children can test the plausibility of long-term predisposing effects more directly.

In perhaps the first longitudinal study on this topic, initiated in 1960 on 856 youth in New York State, Eron, Huesmann, Lefkowitz, and Walder found that boys' early childhood viewing of violence on TV was statistically related to their aggressive and antisocial behavior 10 years later (after graduating from high school) even after initial aggressiveness, social class, education, and other relevant variables were controlled.

A 22-year follow-up of these same boys revealed that their early aggression predicted later criminality at age 30 and that early violence viewing also was independently but weakly related to their adult criminality. A more representative longitudinal study was initiated by Huesmann and his colleagues in 1977. The TV habits of children as young as first graders also predicted subsequent childhood aggression even after initial levels of aggression were controlled. In contrast to earlier longitudinal studies, this effect was obtained for both boys and girls even in countries without large amounts of violent programming, such as Israel, Finland, and Poland.

In most countries, the more aggressive children also watched more TV, preferred more violent programs, identified more with aggressive characters, and perceived TV violence as more like real life than did the less aggressive children. The combination of extensive exposure to violence coupled with identification with aggressive characters was a particularly potent predictor of subsequent aggression for many children. Still, there were differences among the countries. Although the synchronous correlations were positive in all countries, the longitudinal effect of violence viewing on aggression was not significant for girls in Finland or for all children in Australia. In Israel, there were significant effects for children living in a city but not for children raised on a kibbutz.

A few longitudinal studies have seemed to produce results at odds with the thesis that media-violence viewing causes aggression, but closer inspection of most of these studies reveals that their results are not discrepant but simply not strongly supportive of the thesis. For example, although the National Broadcasting Company's longitudinal study of middle-childhood youth conducted in the 1970s reported significant regression coefficients for only 2 out of the 15 critical tests of the causal theory for boys, an additional 10 were in the predicted direction. Furthermore, for girls, 3 out of the 15 critical tests were significant and an additional 7 were in the predicted direction.

Media and Child Rights

There are deep concerns all over the world about the too easy access of young people, especially very young children, to programmes showing needless violence, sex and pornography. This is contrary to the Rights of the Child as set out in the UN Convention, which states in Article 3 that in all actions concerning children the best interests of the child shall be a primary consideration.

Other principles - which should be recognised by the media - are that the opinions of children themselves should be heard. That not only their survival but also their development should be ensured. Finally, that there should be no discrimination between children; each child should be able to enjoy his/her rights, which might include special needs for that child.

The relevant articles are as follows:

1. Each child must have access to information and material from a diversity of national and international sources, especially those aimed at the promotion of his or her social, spiritual and moral well-being and physical and mental health, and
2. the child must receive care and protection as is necessary for his or her well-being
3. mass media must be encouraged to disseminate information and material of social and cultural benefit to the child
4. These rights need to be balanced with children's right to freedom of expression. This right includes the freedom to see, receive and impart information and ideas of all kinds (subject to the protection of public health and morals, and respect of the rights or reputations of others)

Children who watch television are not only entertained but assume, consciously or unconsciously, that they are learning more about the world they live in, who they are in that world and how they should behave. If they take their role models from "The Bold and the Beautiful" they may think that family relationships are all about violence and sex. If they take Power Rangers as an ideal, they may assume that violence solves problems.

World-wide there are not enough local, relevant programmes that affirm the identity of children and help them to learn social and moral values, and the life-skills they need to know that day.

The media, especially newspapers, radio and television, are powerful tools in raising awareness or as partners in an advocacy campaign to promote children's rights. Children make for interesting and appealing stories, and the media is usually sympathetic to their needs.

When the media are involved, we naturally try to make sure that children themselves participate and have a voice, as is their right. But we need to be aware that the media tends to sensationalise any story, and this might conflict with the child's right to privacy and respect. Publicity may also endanger the child's right to safety, protection and development - the child may become a target for violence, for example, if the community feels that he or she has shown them in a bad light.

There is a particular danger when child survivors of violence or ill-treatment or neglect are photographed or interviewed by the Press, radio or television, as there is then a permanent record that may haunt the child for the rest of his or her life.

Good publicity can affirm children in their identity as worthwhile human beings and give them their right to have a say in decisions that affect them. But if a child is given celebrity status this can be difficult to adjust to in every day life! De-briefing is always needed after an exciting event. Children should also not be picked up and then dropped as if they were toys - opportunities for them to be seen and heard should be on-going even if these events are not always on the public stage.

Suggested steps in getting responsible media coverage:

1. Cultivate relationships with trusted reporters and brief them on children's rights and needs so that they become partners in awareness-raising.
2. Provide reporters with guidelines (or training) on what children need and want from the media and the role of the media in building a child-friendly society.
3. Give plenty of notice of "human interest" events that are coming up.
4. Provide background information on the event or issue (perhaps a fact-sheet), that includes the child rights context.
5. Brief children and their guardians about the event and possible media coverage, and get permission for children to be interviewed and photographed, promising that an adult will be present at all times.
6. If children will be drawing or writing for the event, obtain permission from them and their guardians for use to be made of this material, explaining how it will be used and for what purpose.
7. If an article is being written about children who have been interviewed, ask that the children themselves be allowed to see and vet the draft copy before it is printed.

8. Make sure that children do see the final printed article, or hear themselves on radio or watch the TV shot that they were involved with, and have a chance to comment on it.
9. It is important to "de-brief" children and to make sure that the children are comfortable and happy about the media coverage. If they are not, find opportunities to help them to discuss and work through any unhappy experiences. Celebrating successes and planning to do it better next time is always a good way to de-brief.
10. Give children a voice in criticising, or praising, the media if they wish.

Role of Media in Protecting Child Rights

Growing concern about rights of children at national and international governmental level has in recent years tested the resolve of governments to implement international agreements designed to end the exploitation of children. The UN Convention on the Rights of the Child is already the most widely recognised of any international agreement. Concern over child labour, child prostitution and the civil rights of children are a benchmark by which any nation's commitment to human rights and democracy can be judged.

Raising awareness about the rights of children and the promotion of children's rights is a challenge to media and those who work in journalism. Media must not just report fairly, honestly and accurately on the experience of childhood, but they must also provide space for the diverse, colourful and creative opinions of children themselves.

But respect for childrens' rights is not guaranteed by goodwill alone. The pressures of commercial development, cultural diversity and a global economy that gives easy access for a rich minority to regions where people are struggling to emerge from appalling conditions of poverty and colonial exploitation all continue to define the process by which child rights are implemented.

Child sex tourism is one area particularly recognised as requiring greater action at international and regional level. The role of media is crucial in promoting travel and the richness of the tourism industry. Tourism is the world's leading economic sector and this means that all countries compete to lure visitors. The problem is that in many regions, particularly South Asia and South East Asia, sexual exploitation and particularly the exploitation of children is an unpleasant by-product of the explosion in tourism.

It is an issue that involves many players - journalists and media, travel agents and tourism companies, airlines and travel services, hotel and restaurants and entertainment providers. Until now, there has been little co-operation between these different players in seeking to raise awareness on the issue and in taking practical steps to combat the form of exploitation.

Journalists themselves are too often ignorant of child rights issues and unaware of how media contribute, often unknowingly, to the commercial process that encourages sexual exploitation of children. Research have shown that existing efforts to combat child sex tourism are virtually unknown inside journalism. The existence of the World Tourism Organisation Globe Code of Ethics for Tourism, for instance, which was adopted in Chile in, remains largely unknown inside journalism. The WTO code states:

Article 2 (2)

> "Tourism activities should respect the equality of men and women; they should promote human rights and, more particularly, the individual rights of the most vulnerable groups, notably children..."

Article 2 (3)

> The exploitation of human beings in any form, particularly sexual, especially when applied to children, conflicts with the fundamental aims of tourism and is the negation of tourism, as such, in accordance with international law, it should be energetically combated...and penalised without concession by the national legislation of both the countries visited and countries of the perpetrators of these acts, even when they are carried out abroad."

The International Federation of Journalists (IFJ) and its member organisations also have spent some time in framing guidelines for journalists that set out practical lines of professional action and consideration in the area of child rights. These guidelines were originally adopted at a world conference in Brazil in 1998 and endorsed at the IFJ congress in Seoul in 2001. More than 100 journalists organizations have committed themselves to the code.

Whether it is news and current affairs, or the more complex world of the creative and performing arts, all media professionals and the organisations for which they work have a responsibility to recognise that children's rights concern them. But how do we raise awareness? To answer this question requires serious examination of the way media work, of how existing principles of accountability apply, and how media must be freed from reins of political and economic control which limit professionalism and undermine ethical standards.

Irrespective of external pressure, the media's role in the evolution of children's rights is complex. On the one hand, news media tell the stories of abused and abuser, through news reports, photographs, documentaries, and drama. But on the other, they can themselves become the exploiter, for instance by creating sexually provocative images of children in news or advertising, or, at worst, as the vehicle for child pornography, or sources of information for pedophile networks, something of particular concern in the age of Internet. Furthermore, the way the media portray children has a profound impact on society's attitude to children and childhood, which also affects the way adults behave.

Media professionals need to consider these questions, even if there are no easy answers to complex issues or to ethical dilemmas. There are standards and benchmarks by which media can judge how they portray children in society. In the conclusion of this section are a number of practical recommendations intended to make media and journalists more responsive and to encourage debate within media about the portrayal of children and their rights.

Looking particularly at child sex tourism, internal editorial arrangements within media sometimes are sometimes an obstacle to good coverage and better understanding of issues. Journalists need to be aware of the consequences of their reporting and their role in safeguarding the rights and the dignity of children and young adults. Sensational coverage often distorts and exploits a serious problem, perhaps doing more harm than good, but often the response of editors will be that they are trying to fulfill the responsibility to cover serious social issues, while continuing to turn a profit. Sensationalism, they argue, permits an important but unpleasant topic to be covered in such a way that it still captures the readers' and viewers' attention. However, such coverage rarely analyses the social and economic causes of abuse of children: the dislocation of communities and families, homelessness, the effects of conflict, corrupt employers, child traffickers, pimps, the drug culture or why parents in poverty sell a child to support the rest of the family.

Nevertheless, media can broaden the scope of reporting. The positive story of children, their lives and their rights is not being told in full. To examine how this can be changed requires examination of the professional conditions in which media work, a review of the principles or guidelines journalists and programme-makers should follow, and the obstacles - legal, financial, or cultural - that stand in the way of good journalism.

A starting point for good reporting is freedom of information. Journalists are only ever as good as their sources of information. Reporting on child rights requires access to a great deal of information about children, much of it held by the state authorities. Media cannot report effectively if information about education, health, employment, development and social conditions is not made generally available. In too many countries, governments and state institutions are secretive and hoard information. Citizens have a right to freedom of information. Without it, media cannot report accurately on the reality of children's lives. Also, journalists and NGOs need a better understanding of each other's roles to foster greater cooperation. An effective media liaison service will ensure that media has access to reliable sources of information on children's issues.

Respect, too, for independent journalism is an essential condition for a media culture of openness about children and their rights. For example, journalists recognise that betraying sources not only inhibits their own ability to investigate; it also makes it more difficult for every journalist to work, and may even put their lives at risk, as well as the safety of the informants. Many of the professional obligations of journalists are set out in codes of professional conduct. But how effective are voluntary codes and guidelines? The simple answer is the same as that for all forms of self-regulation - it depends upon the professional confidence of journalists, their knowledge of the issues they are dealing with, and the conditions in which they work.

The worldwide study of codes reveals that journalists' organisations until recently had few specific codes of good practice for covering the rights of children. To remedy this in May 1998 the International Federation of Journalists launched the first international guidelines for journalists covering children's rights at a conference attended by journalists from 70 countries. Regional discussion on these guidelines followed in Latin America and Africa and the guidelines were endorsed by the full meeting of the IFJ congress in Asia in 2001.

The aim of this code - which is attached to this section - is to ensure accuracy and sensitivity among journalists when reporting on issues involving children. The code gets to the core of people's concerns when it comes to how media deal with the children, including:

— sexual, violent or victim-focused programming and images that are potentially damaging to children;

— stereotypes and sensational presentation of journalistic material;

— media failure to consider the consequences of publication and to minimise harm to children;

— respect for the privacy of children and protection of their identity unless it is demonstrably in the public interest;

— the need to give children access to media to express their own opinions;

— the obligation to verify information before publication.

The challenge to journalists and media in addressing these problems is to be aware of their responsibilities and to promote improvements. While codes cannot guarantee ethical reporting, they do identify the professional dilemmas that journalists and media face when reporting on the rights of children.

Fierce commercial competition is one factor leading media to exploit victims. The exposure of emotions and sensationalisation of events attract audiences and sell news. Cash-conscious media organisations apply greater pressure on news teams for productivity. Journalists, therefore, sometimes take the ill-considered, easy route to newsgathering, perpetuating the sorts of myth and stereotype identified above.

But in all this there are many examples of good journalism that act as a counter-weight to media indifference and lack of awareness. There is a need for media to identify good practice, to applaud high standards and to encourage improved coverage. Journalism prizes, organised at national, regional and international level can do much if they are used to stimulate debate and dialogue.

Media professionals need to develop strategies that strengthen the role of media in providing information on all aspects of the children's rights, but particularly dealing with child sex tourism. The following recommendations are designed to raise awareness about the importance of this issue:

1. Training for journalists and Media Education

    a) Materials outlining the Convention on the Rights of the Child and ILO Convention 182 on the worst forms of child labour, and their implications for media as well as examples of good practice within media can form the basis of training courses and manuals for journalists and other media professionals.

    b) Training seminars looking at the professional challenges for journalists, including interviewing, taking photographs and using images, including children's voices.

    c) Training seminars focused on issues related to commercial sexual exploitation of children and trafficking of children should be organised to raise awareness within media of these issues.

2. Creating the Conditions for Professional Journalism

    a) Industry partners, workforce representatives and tourism authorities should work with media and other civil society groups to create the conditions for legitimate journalistic inquiry and monitoring of how children can be adversely affected by tourism arrangements.

    b) Media professionals should recognise that freedom of expression must go hand in hand with other fundamental human rights, including freedom from exploitation and intimidation. They should give careful consideration to the facts when weighing up the relative merits of the different claims, and not allow themselves to be swayed by commercial or political considerations;

c) Dialogue between media organisations, journalists, the tourism workforce, police and NGOs should be supported to highlight problems and concerns and better understanding of the needs of journalists and media when reporting on exploitation of children.

d) A process of regular review of Codes of Ethics and Journalistic Guidelines to ensure that they are effective and enforced.

e) National NGOs, government, unions and industry representatives should consider compiling a directory of reliable experts on the rights of children and related topics, to be distributed to media. Such information could also be accessible on computer data banks.

3. Codes of Conduct and Self-Regulation

a) Codes of conduct and reporting guidelines can be useful in demonstrating that something needs to be done. Specific guidelines on child rights reporting, such as those adopted by the IFJ, should be drawn up by professional associations to accom- pany their general ethical codes and should draw attention to issues regarding vio- lence against children and commercial sexual exploitation.

b) Journalists and programme-makers have a duty to increase public awareness of the violation of children's rights. However, reporting needs to be carried out with enormous care. In particular, media should adhere to the highest standards of professional conduct when reporting on the rights of children.

c) They should avoid, or challenge, the myths and stereotypes that surround children, particularly those from developing countries. For instance, the myth that parents in developing countries do not value their children; that girls are inferior to boys; that children are drawn into crime through their own fault; or that child labour and sex tourism alleviate poverty for the victim, or the host nation.

d) Journalists should never publish details that put vulnerable children at risk. Journalists should take particular care not to reveal information that damages the dignity of children, and avoid identifying them, while at the same time telling their stories in a compelling and newsworthy way.

4. The Need for Newsroom Debate

a) A constructive and supportive debate should be encouraged between media professionals, about reporting of children's rights and media images of children. Such dialogue should take place between media managements, journalists and other media professionals and marketing sections.

2

Impact of Media on Child Education

Media has many definitions ranging from "a particular form of communication" as in 'print versus video' to "the industry that provides news and entertainment" as in 'the media'. It can also be defined as "all means of communication, whatever its format." In this sense, media include symbol systems as diverse as print, graphics, animation, audio, and motion pictures. Similarly, technology has many definitions ranging from "the application of the scientific method to solve problems as in 'the technology of space exploration'" to "the things or processes which embody knowledge or craft within a culture as in 'the technology of writing'." Technology can be defined as "any object or process of human origin that can be used to convey media." In this sense, technology includes phenomena as diverse as books, films, television, and the Internet.

Media and technology have been introduced into schools because it is believed that they can have positive effects on teaching and learning. With respect to education, media are the symbol systems that teachers and students use to represent knowledge; technologies are the tools that allow them to share their knowledge representations with others. Unfortunately, it is common for practitioners and experts alike to confound the meanings of media and technology in education, and they are often used synonymously. The following quote from the Fifth Edition of the Encyclopedia of Educational Research illustrates the problem:

> "First, although most educators are comfortable enough to use the term "media" and expect others to understand its meaning, it lacks a commonly accepted definition. Instead, there is a general, somewhat vague understanding that it refers to various audio and/or visual communication technologies which have come to be used by educators. Books and other print materials are, of course, media too, yet it is usually understood from the context - including the present context - that they are not part of the topic under discussion."

The confounding of media (a symbol system) with technology (a delivery system for media) is unlikely to go away in popular discourse about education any time soon, but the distinction between media and technology must be clarified as unambiguously as possible if their impact is to be understood. The following quote from the Sixth Edition of the Encyclopedia of Educational Research clarifies this distinction:

> Computer-based technologies cannot be regarded as "media," because the variety of programs, tools, and devices that can be used with them is neither limited to a particular symbol system, nor to a particular class of activities...... In this light, "the computer" is in fact a "multifaceted invention" of many uses, a symbolic tool for making, exploring, and thinking in various domains. It is used to represent and manipulate symbol systems - language, mathematics,

music - and to create symbolic products - poems, mathematical proofs, compositions.

With respect to media, there are many issues of concern to students, parents, educators, governments, and society at large. For example, important questions are asked about the effects of different media on the cognitive and moral development of children. With respect to technology, people want to know whether various new technologies are more effective for teaching and learning than more traditional classroom approaches, whether some technologies are more motivating than others, or at the very least, whether technologies can be used to increase access or reduce costs within education.

Questions about the impact of media and technology in terms of increasing access to education and reducing the costs of education are especially high on the agendas of politicians and government agencies around the world. In the USA, the Panel of Educational Technology of the President's Committee of Advisors on Science and Technology included as one of its six major strategic recommendations that technology be used to "Ensure equitable, universal access". Another part of the same report called for realistic budgeting for technology-related expenditures within schools, noting that the much-touted return-on-investment for educational technology was a long-term prospect.

Another reason for the attention being paid to media and technology in education reflects commercial or corporate interests. Although printed material continues to be "the dominant medium format" in schools, a recent Presidential report in the USA recommends that "at least five percent of all public K-12 educational spending in the United States should be earmarked for technology-related expenditures...." Similar investments are underway throughout the world, in both developed and developing countries. It is no wonder that global corporations such as AT&T and Sony are investing in large-scale educational technology initiatives.

Still another reason for the focus on media and education stems from sharp disagreements about the value of media and technology in education. Enthusiastic endorsements of new media and technologies in education are easy to find in news reports, political speeches, and other sources. Many of these proclamations seem overly-optimistic if not hyperbolic. Consider this quote from Lewis Perelman's 1993 book titled School's Out:

> Because of the pervasive and potent impact of HL (hyperlearning) technology, we now are experiencing the turbulent advent of an economic and social transformation more profound than the industrial revolution. The same technology that is transforming work offers new learning systems to solve the problems it creates. In the wake of the HL revolution, the technology called "school" and the social institution commonly thought of as "education" will be as obsolete and ultimately extinct as the dinosaurs.

However, despite such rhetoric and other, more conservative, optimism expressed in the popular press and government documents, there are also many skeptics and a few outspoken critics of media and technology in education. A recent cover story of The Atlantic Monthly entitled "The Computer Delusion" illustrates a critical view of technology in education, beginning with this opening sentence:

> There is no good evidence that most uses of computers significantly improve teaching and learning, yet school districts are cutting programs - music, art, physical

education - that enrich children's lives to make room for this dubious nostrum, and the Clinton Administration has embraced the goal of "computers in every classroom" with credulous and costly enthusiasm.

The controversy in the popular press is echoed in the educational research literature. Research examining the effectiveness of media and technology in schools can be traced back almost eighty years, and yet many questions about the value and impact of these approaches remain unanswered. Indeed, the seemingly contradictory findings often reported in the educational research literature fan the flames of the ongoing controversy about media and technology in education.

Bringing the electronic media into the schools could capitalize on the strong motivation qualities that these media have for children. Many children who are turned off by school are not turned off by one or another of the electronic media; quite the opposite. An educational system that capitalized on this motivation would have a chance of much greater success. Each medium has its own profile of cognitive advantages and disadvantages, and each medium can be used to enhance the impact of others.

All in all, media's symbolic forms and computers' afforded activities often have skill-cultivating effects. However, to claim that these effects are specific to any one medium or media attribute is difficult. There is growing consensus that past media comparison, media attribute, and motivation studies indicate that media do not influence whether someone learns from instruction. Learning seems to result from factors such as task differences, instructional methods, and learner traits but not the choice of media for instruction.

Approaches to Using Media/Technology in Schools

There are two major approaches to using media and technology in schools: students can learn "from" media and technology, and they can learn "with" media and technology. Learning "from" media and technology is often referred to in terms such as instructional television, computer-based instruction, or integrated learning systems. Learning "with" technology, less widespread than the "from" approach, is referred to in terms such as cognitive tools and constructivist learning environments. Regardless of the approach, media and technology have been introduced into schools because it is believed that they can have positive effects on teaching and learning.

Learning "From" Media and Technology

The foundation for the use of media and technology as "tutors" in schools is "educational communications," i.e., the deliberate and intentional act of communicating content to students with the assumption that they will learn something "from" these communications. In educational communications, information or knowledge is encoded visually or verbally in the symbol systems (media) that are enabled by various technologies. For example, animation is a form of media that can be delivered to students via a variety of technologies such as the World Wide Web. Within a web-based science tutorial, an animation of the movement of the moon around the earth might be shown to students so that they can visualize and learn about the lunar phases.

The instructional processes inherent in the "from" approach to using media and technology in schools usually can be reduced to a series of simple steps:

1) exposing students to messages encoded in media and delivered by technology,
2) assuming that students perceive and encode these messages,
3) requiring a response to indicate that messages have been received, and
4) providing feedback as to the adequacy of the response.

Interaction in the "from" approach, if present, is normally operationalized in terms of student input via the technology such as clicking a mouse button to indicate a response to a multiple-choice question, some form of answer judging, and feedback in the form of another message previously encoded in the media. Instructional technologies (e.g., films and teaching machines) were first introduced early in this century in the belief that they could "teach" in a similar sense that teachers or tutors are said to teach.

Let us consider the two most widely used forms of media and technology—television and computers—as tutors.

Television as Tutor

Since the first educational television broadcasts began in Iowa in 1933, there have been decades of research focused on the educational effects of television, and yet controversies about the impact of television in schools and society as a whole persist. For example, some well-known social critics maintain that television viewing is cognitively debilitating.

A review of the television research literature, however, indicates that such claims are largely based upon subjective observations rather than theory-guided investigations, and there is no conclusive evidence that television stultifies the mind. There is also no consistent evidence that television increases either hyperactivity or passivity in children.

Another popular belief is that television viewing is detrimental to the academic achievement of school-age children and teens. While some studies have reported a negative correlation between the amount of television viewing and scholastic performance, such statistics are susceptible to misinterpretations because of intervening variables such as intelligence and socioeconomic status.

In a book titled *Literacy in the Television Age: The Myth of the TV Effect*, Susan Neuman provides an in-depth review of research examining the relationship between television and achievement. She concludes that there is insufficient support for the hypothesis that television viewing displaces academic activities such as reading or homework and thereby has a negative impact on school achievement.

A competing analysis of the literature by Comstock and Paik concluded that the relationship between the amount of time spent viewing television and achievement test scores (primarily reading tests) is curvilinear with achievement actually rising with 1-2 hours of television per day, but gradually falling with longer daily viewing periods.

Undoubtedly, the most widespread belief about television is that it fosters violence and aggressive behaviors among children and adolescents. A survey of the literature indicates that there have been nearly 20 books published on this topic in the last decade alone, most of them condemning television as causing aggression. In addition, scores of research studies related to this topic are published around the world each year.

There is little disagreement that in many, if not most, countries television provides a steady flow of violence ranging to as many as 25 violent acts per hour in children's programming. The preponderance of the quantitative research evidence indicates that viewing violence on television is moderately correlated with aggression in children and adolescents, but as with all such correlational research, the evidence for direct causality is weaker.

Alternative explanations for the reported correlations are possible, e.g., those children with a tendency toward aggression may be more likely to watch violent television programs. Despite the weak evidence for causality, both the public in general and many politicians have come to accept the conclusion that television violence has negative effects on youth. As a result, legislation has recently been passed in the USA to compel television networks to provide violence ratings for their programs and to require manufacturers to install electronic blocking devices (such as the "V-chip") in new TV sets. Similar laws are already in place in other countries.

Less publicized than hypotheses about the negative effects of television on cognitive development, scholastic achievement, and social behavior are research investigations into the positive effects of television viewing on factors such as interest, creativity, and imagination. Howard Gardner, a well-known developmental psychologist at Harvard University, is a proponent of the idea that certain kinds of television stimulate creativity and imagination in young children. However, the research results supporting these types of positive hypotheses are modest at best.

Let us consider some exemplary programs aimed to educate children. Two television shows that have been subjected to more educational research than any others in the USA are Mister Rogers' Neighborhood and Sesame Street, both shown on public television stations. Sesame Street, distributed in more than 90 countries, has also been studied internationally.

The goals of Mister Rogers' Neighborhood are primary affective, and research has demonstrated positive effects on the self-esteem of children and their tendencies to value others. With emphasis on both socialization and cognitive development, Sesame Street has been shown to have positive outcomes in terms of school readiness as well as math, reading, and social skills. Interestingly, some researchers have focused on whether the slower-paced Mister Rogers' Neighborhood and the faster-paced Sesame Street have differential effects on children's attention spans, but such studies are inconclusive.

The most positive research news about learning "from" television can be found in the classroom where 40 years of research show positive effects on learning from television programs that are explicitly produced and used for instructional purposes. In addition, most studies show that there are no significant differences in effectiveness between live teacher presentations and videos of teacher presentations.

There is strong evidence that television is used most effectively when it is intentionally designed for education and when teachers are involved in its selection, utilization, and integration into the curriculum. In the past, the biggest barrier to the integration of television programs into the classroom was the fixed-time limitation of instructional broadcasts, but the wide-spread availability of video cassette recorders (VCRs) has provided teachers with the ease-of-use and flexibility they require.

Increasingly, television is coming into schools via cable and or satellite transmissions. The Star Schools Consortium in the USA is one of the largest such enterprises, providing scores of telecourses in thousands of schools across the nation. Most often, programs received via satellite dish or cable are recorded by media specialists or technology coordinators and subsequently made available for teachers when and how they choose. Flexibility of scheduling and ease of access to equipment and programs are the biggest factors promoting classroom use of television.

A few programs are still intended for use at specific times. Perhaps the most controversial of these in the USA is Channel One, ten minutes of news and advertisements produced by Whittle Communications. This program is seen by an estimated eight million adolescents in 12,000 schools in the USA each day. CNN, NBC, and other networks broadcast news into American classrooms, but Channel One is best known for the contracts it arranges with school districts whereby Whittle donates TV monitors and satellite receivers to schools in return for guaranteed viewing time each school day. Whittle recovers its costs from the fees it charges corporations for product advertisements aimed at the captive teen viewers. Interestingly, what little research has been done indicates that students ignore the advertisements and that teachers are not integrating the news portions of the program into the curriculum.

Historically, studies of the large-scale implementations of instructional television have shown mixed results. Three major forms of utilization have been investigated:

1) instances where the total instructional program is delivered via televised teachers,

2) instances where there is an integration of teacher-directed instruction with television programming, and

3) instances where television is used to supplement teacher-centered instruction, either for enrichment or remedial purposes.

Some research studied have pointed out that total instructional television programs in countries such as American Samoa and El Salvador have met with initial enthusiasm, but declined in popularity after the novelty wore off and both students and teachers demanded less television and a return to regular classroom activities. Some studies indicate that students in rural schools, where quality teachers were less likely to be available, benefited the most from televised instruction.

However, television has been rarely used to totally replace teachers in any country, and television is usually used in coordination with or to supplement the regular curriculum. Here the results are much more positive. A large-scale survey of teachers in the USA conducted in 1991 by the Corporation for Public Broadcasting indicated that "instructional television is a firmly established teaching tool that is positively regarded by classroom teachers and increasingly well-supported with equipment and programming".

Unfortunately, there is a paucity of developmental research focused on how teachers might best use television in the classroom to enhance academic achievement. We know that motivation is an important factor in gaining the most from any educational experience, but we don't know how teachers can effectively motivate students to attend to educational television. We know that feedback concerning the message received (or not received) from television is important, but we lack clear directions as to when and how teachers should provide that feedback. And even when recommendations for using television in the classroom do exist, there is little evidence that these guidelines are integral parts of the curriculum in most teacher preparation programs.

According to a recent survey most children in the USA view less than 30 minutes of television a week in school whereas their home televisions are on nearly seven hours per day! Why isn't television used more widely in education? The teacher plays the major role in deciding what happens in the classroom, and as long as teachers experience difficulty in previewing videos, obtaining equipment, incorporating programs into the curriculum, and linking television programming to assessment activities, television viewing will continue to be relatively rare in classrooms. It also seems likely that the widespread public belief that television has detrimental effects on development, learning, and behavior will continue to limit television integration within most classrooms beyond that of a relatively modest supplementary role.

Computer as Tutor

The personal computer is the most common interactive technology used as a "tutor" today. Interactive instruction via personal computer is known by many names and acronyms such as computer-based instruction (CBI), integrated learning systems (ILS), and intelligent tutoring systems (ITS). The personal computer as a tutor or surrogate instructor has been the subject for much research and evaluation since its development in the late 1970s. Critics of computers as tutors have been around since their inception, and there are vocal opponents of computers in classrooms today.

One irony underlying research on learning from computers is that while everyone recognizes the amazing improvements in the features and capabilities of personal computers that have occurred in the past 20 years, few people outside the research community acknowledge that the nature of computer-based learning has also undergone enormous change.

The earliest forms of computer-based instruction were heavily influenced by the behavioral psychology of B.F. Skinner. These programs were essentially automated forms of programmed instruction. They presented information to the student in small segments, required the student to make overt responses to the information as stimulus, and provided feedback to the student along with differential branching to other segments of instruction or to drill-and-practice routines. Although this basic behavioral model continues to dominate mainstream educational applications of computers such as integrated learning systems, interactivity in some of today's most innovative applications, such as constructivist learning environments, is based upon advances in cognitive psychology and constructivist pedagogy.

The good news is that even with a primarily behavioral pedagogy, computers as tutors have positive effects on learning as measured by standardized achievement tests, are more motivating for students, are accepted by more teachers than other technologies, and are widely supported by administrators, parents, politicians, and the public in general. These conclusions about the effectiveness of computers in classrooms in the USA are in agreement with the conclusions of similar reports in Australia, Canada, and the United Kingdom. Regrettably, the impacts of CBI in countries such as Brazil, Chile, China, and Malaysia are less clear.

Meta-analyses of research examining the effectiveness of computers in schools have illuminated their advantages and limitations. Meta-analysis is a statistical procedure that allows researchers to synthesize the results of numerous research studies comparing different treatments (e.g., CBI versus teacher-centered instruction) by reducing the results to a common "effect size".

Although some proponents of computer-based instruction have promised a 2.0 effect size (representing an improvement of two standard deviations between CBI and traditional instruction), a more reasonable expectation is in the range of 0.5 to 1.0. The results of meta-analyses for computer-based instruction show an interesting pattern.

The effectiveness of CBI over traditional teacher-centered instructional methods appears to decline as the level of education increases with the exception of adult basic education, where CBI has an effect size between that of secondary and elementary school contexts.

A variety of explanations have been offered for these differential effects ranging from the belief that teachers in lower grades are better at integrating CBI into the curriculum to the suggestion that there is less well-designed software available in the higher grades. Clark maintains that media and technology are mere vehicles for instructional methods. He provides an alternative interpretation of the differential effect sizes by arguing that when the differences in pedagogy are factored out of the comparisons between CBI and teacher-centered instruction, the effect sizes virtually disappear.

A more robust finding for computer-based instruction is that students are able to complete a given set of educational objectives in less time with CBI than needed in more traditional approaches. The time savings factor was first identified in military training contexts where a consistent 25% to 50% reduction in time to train has been demonstrated when interactive technologies are employed. The pressure to save instructional time has not been as great in school contexts, a situation that may change if proponents of national assessments are successful, and teachers perceive the need to cover more content within the school year.

Given the positive results for the computer as tutor approach, some questions can be asked about the relative effectiveness of different approaches to instructional computing in classrooms. There two major major tutorial approaches: integrated learning systems (ILS) and intelligent tutoring systems (ITS).

Integrated learning systems (ILS): Integrated learning systems (ILS) utilize computer networks to combine comprehensive educational "courseware" with centralized management tools. ILS are marketed by large commercial vendors such as Computer Curriculum Corporation (CCC) and Jostens Learning Corporation. CCC's programs are reported to be in use by millions of students in 16,000 classrooms in the USA, Canada, UK, Japan, Australia, and New Zealand. Jostens claims that its courseware is used by 9 million students in 13,000 schools around the world.

There were approximately a dozen major ILS vendors in the early 1990s, although recent mergers indicate that a market shake-out is underway. Bailey and Becker describe some of the perceived advantages of integrated learning systems that help to explain why ILS dominate the school technology market:

— Networking allows centralized management by teachers and administrators.

— Diagnostic and prescriptive analysis techniques built into ILS provide the basis for more and better individualization of lesson materials for students.

— The logistical problems associated with software distribution and maintenance are eliminated by networking from centralized servers.

— Strong tutorials and extensive drill-and-practice opportunities are provided for students within a wide range of abilities.

— There is an obvious articulation between the content of ILS lessons and standardized assessment approaches used in most schools.

— Students and teachers can experience a common user interface across subjects and grades.

ILS are complex systems that involve the use of specific hardware and software to address large portions of the standard school curriculum, especially in areas such as mathematics, reading, and language arts. Funding for the development of early versions of these systems came from government resources targeted for "at risk" students, and they are sometimes criticized as having too much "drill and kill" materials in them.

Becker provides evidence that ILS are most effective for those students with either low or high aptitude for regular classroom instruction, but that the 40% of students in the middle range experience no improvement from ILS over regular classroom instruction. Becker uses meta-analysis techniques to examine the effectiveness of some of the ILS from major vendors. Most of the results are positive, but much more modest than promised by the vendors themselves.

Despite the lack of evidence that ILS are as effective as the commercial interests behind them claim, they are quite likely to play an even larger role in classrooms in the foreseeable future. For example, a January 1998 press release indicates that Jostens Learning has initiated a seven-year partnership with Addison-Wesley Longman, one of the world's largest education publishers, to promote ILS in the United Kingdom where a new government initiative aims at increasing the use of technology in schools. The collaboration predicts at least a 34 million dollar contract within the UK alone. In November 1997, Computer Curriculum Corporation inked a reported 50 million dollar agreement with Research Machines, the leading supplier of educational software in the UK. Investors in these companies are confident in a bright future for ILS.

To their credit, most of the ILS on the market have been redesigned in recent years to take advantage of multimedia capabilities and advances in instructional design. Unfortunately, the new versions of ILS have not been subjected to rigorous research and evaluation studies. The WWW sites associated with ILS vendors contain both testimonials and anecdotal evidence, but there is a complete lack of large-scale, externally conducted, rigorous research studies reported in the sites or obtainable through public information resources such as ERIC (Educational Resources Information Clearinghouse). In addition, there is evidence that vendors underestimate the training required for teachers to make effective use of ILS or other forms of software.

Intelligent Tutoring Systems (ITS): The basic components of ITS were conceptualized 25 years ago as:

1) knowledge of the domain,
2) knowledge of the learner, and
3) knowledge of teaching strategies.

In ITS language, these are often referred to as the expert model, the student model, and the tutor. Others trace the history of ITS all the way back to 1926 when Sidney L. Pressey built an "instructional machine" that presented a student with multiple-choice questions, a device which could even dispense candy for correct answers. Advocates of ITS promote these systems as "the most promising approach to delivering individualized instruction" because the "artificial intelligence" aspects of the program can allegedly diagnose and remedy student misconceptions with the precision of a human tutor.

Although much of the development of ITS has been done in the context of military and industrial training, there have been significant efforts to develop ITS for education, especially in challenging subjects such as algebra, calculus, and programming. For example, John Anderson is well known for his work building a geometry ITS. An evaluation of Anderson's geometry tutor in an urban school setting indicated that the system had both positive learning outcomes and encouraged more cooperative problem-solving among students.

Unfortunately, despite a few positive evaluations in loosely controlled studies, few ITS have demonstrated the significant results promised by their developers.

ITS attracted much more attention, funding, and research a few years ago than they do today. One telling sign is that the Journal of Artificial Intelligence in Education recently changed its name to the Journal of Interactive Learning Research. Even those who have been most involved in research and development targeted at producing "intelligent tutors" have begun to acknowledge the lack of impact they have had on mainstream education. A major factor contributing to the lack of success of ITS is that the technical difficulties inherent in building student models and facilitating human-like communications have been greatly underestimated by proponents of this approach. In the face of the disappointing results of ITS, some experts suggest that "...the appropriate role for a computer is not that of a teacher/expert, but rather, that of a mind-extension 'cognitive tool'".

Cognitive tools are unintelligent tools, relying on the learner to provide the intelligence, not the computer. This means that planning, decision-making, and self-regulation are the responsibility of the learner, not the technology. Cognitive tools can serve as powerful catalysts for facilitating these higher order skills if they are used in ways that promote reflection, discussion, and collaborative problem-solving.

Research and evaluation of the effectiveness of CBI and other applications of computers as tutors have been plagued by flaws that render much of the existing literature little more than pseudoscience. One reason for this deplorable state of affairs is that there has long been great disagreement about the purpose and value of educational research. For example, Nate Gage, a past president of the American Educational Research Association (AERA), has been a staunch defender of the notion that the goal of basic research in education is simply "more valid and more positive conclusions" whereas another past president of AERA, Robert Ebel, proclaimed:

> ....the value of basic research in education is severely limited, and here is the reason. The process of education is not a natural phenomenon of the kind that has sometimes rewarded scientific investigation. It is not one of the givens in our universe. It is man-made, designed to serve our needs. It is not governed by any natural laws. It is not in need of research to find out how it works. It is in need of creative invention to make it work better.

Despite the increased acceptance of qualitative alternatives to the experimental methods that dominated educational research in the past, there are signs that some powerful policy-makers are pushing for more classically empirical approaches. For example, the Panel of Educational Technology of the President's Committee of Advisors on Science and Technology listed as one of its six major strategic recommendations that the government "initiate a major program of experimental research....to ensure both the efficacy and cost-effectiveness of technology use within our nation's schools". A wiser course would be to support both development research and empirical using both quantitative and qualitative methods.

Learning with Media and Technology

Cognitive tools have been around for thousands of years, ever since primitive humans used piles of stones, marks on trees, and knots in vines to calculate sums or record events. In the broadest sense, cognitive tools refer to technologies, tangible or intangible, that enhance the cognitive powers of human beings during thinking, problem-solving, and learning. Something as complex as a mathematical formula or as simple as a grocery list can be regarded as a cognitive tool in the sense that each allows humans to "off-load" memorization or other mental tasks onto an external resource.

Today, computer software programs are examples of exceptionally powerful cognitive tools. Also referred to as "cognitive technologies", "technologies of the mind", and "mindtools", they will be referred to as "cognitive tools" here. As computers have become more and more common in education, researchers have begun to explore the impact of software as cognitive tools in schools.

Computers as cognitive tools represent quite a different approach from media and technology as vehicles for educational communications. Computer-based cognitive tools have been intentionally adapted or developed to function as intellectual partners to enable and facilitate critical thinking and higher order learning. Examples of cognitive tools include:

- databases,
- spreadsheets,
- semantic networks,
- expert systems,
- communications software such as teleconferencing programs,
- on-line collaborative knowledge construction environments,
- multimedia/hypermedia construction software, and
- computer programming languages.

In the cognitive tools approach, information is not encoded in predefined educational communications which are then used to transmit knowledge to students. Indeed, with cognitive tools, the need for formal instructional systems design processes are reduced.

Instead of specialists such as instructional designers shaping students' learning via prescribed communications and interactions, media and technology are given directly to learners to use for representing and expressing what they know. Learners themselves function as designers using media and technology as tools for analyzing the world, accessing and interpreting information, organizing their personal knowledge, and representing what they know to others.

It is necessary to highlight differences between this new conception and earlier perspectives of using computers and other technologies to support learning that have not been as successful as promised. In 1980, Taylor described the three major roles of computers in education as "tutor, tool, and tutee." The tutor role has enjoyed some success, and promises to be even more successful as cognitive learning theories increasingly guide the design of integrated learning environments and other forms of CBI.

The computer as productivity tool in the sense defined by Taylor has enjoyed some success, especially when used to support writing. However, other software tools such as spreadsheet, database, and computer-aided design (CAD) programs have failed to improve teaching and learning as much as promised by proponents of the technology as tool approach because they have been largely used in the context of traditional "instructivist" pedagogy.

Goodlad described the teacher-directed, text-dominated, curriculum that characterizes most instructional practice in American schools. Ironically, software tools have often been regarded as objects for study in themselves and subjected to the same instructivist pedagogy that limits intellectual growth by students in areas such as science, mathematics, and social studies.

For example, although computer-aided design (CAD) software has revolutionized professional practices and dramatically increased productivity in engineering, architecture, and other design fields, it has had little impact in education. Industrial arts teachers have enthusiastically adopted CAD software into their classrooms and labs, but instead of engaging students in authentic tasks, they often "teach" students the command sets for the software outside of meaningful contexts. Students end up failing to perceive the relevance and value of CAD programs within the design professions or how to apply the software within their own design projects. As pointed out by Salomon, Perkins, and Globerson, "No important impact can be expected when the same old activity is carried out with a technology that makes it a bit faster or easier; the activity itself has to change".

Embraced with almost religious fervor in some circles, the tutee role for computers in education has also delivered less than promised. According to the "tutee" approach, students develop higher order thinking skills and creativity by teaching computers to perform tasks, e.g., draw a picture, using "friendly" programming languages such as Logo and microworlds such as Karel the Robot. Unfortunately, studies aimed at investigating the effects of Logo have failed to demonstrate the cognitive advantages promised by Logo enthusiasts.

Defenders of the "tutee" approach would maintain that the Logo implementations investigated in most studies were too brief and unfocused. Indeed, many applications of Logo described in the literature lack the "mindful engagement" that Salomon and Globerson argue is necessary for learning. More intensive Logo implementations where students are engaged in meaningful tasks over longer periods of time have demonstrated more impressive cognitive effects.

Constructivist Learning Theory

In recent years, learning theory has gone through what can be called a "paradigm shift." Constructivist learning theory is gradually gaining the same respect and attention long accorded to behavioral learning theory. Constructivism concerns the process of how students create meaning and knowledge in the world as well as the results of the constructive process.

How students construct knowledge depends upon what they already know, their previous experiences, how they have organized those experiences into knowledge structures such as schema and mental models, and the beliefs they use to interpret the objects and events they encounter in the world. Cognitive tools help learners organize, restructure, and represent what they know.

For constructivists, the ultimate nature of reality does not matter as much as its local nature, i.e., learners' unique and shared constructions of reality. According to constructivism, a teacher cannot map his/her own interpretations of the world onto learners because they do not share a set of common experiences and interpretations.

"Reality" resides in the mind of each knower who interprets the external world according to his/her own experiences, beliefs, and knowledge. Learners are able to comprehend a variety of interpretations and to use them in arriving at their own unique interpretations of the world. The mind filters input from the world in making its interpretations, and therefore each learner conceives of the external world somewhat differently.

Whereas instructivists emphasize the transmission of standardized interpretations of the world by teachers and the educational media and technology they use as well as standardized assessments to test the degree to which students' understandings match accepted interpretations, constructivists seek to create learning environments wherein learners use cognitive tools to help themselves construct their own knowledge representations. Cognitive tools and the goals, tasks, pedagogies, resources, and human collaboration integral to their use enable learners to engage in active, mindful, and purposeful interpretation and reflection.

Learners as Designers

Following the maxim that the surest way to learn something is to teach it to others, the process of designing instructional materials enables instructional designers to understand content much more deeply than the students whose thinking will be constrained and controlled by the very materials they are developing. It follows that empowering learners to design and produce their own knowledge representations and educational communications can be a powerful learning experience.

Langer reminded us of the importance of mindfulness in learning. Students learn and retain the most from thinking in meaningful ways. Representing knowledge is a mindful task that can be enabled by cognitive tools such as multimedia construction software or electronic spreadsheets.

Cognitive tools require students to think in meaningful ways about how to use an application's capabilities and features to represent what they know. Students not only learn deeply and mindfully with cognitive tools, their opportunities for reflection are also enhanced. There is considerable evidence that reflective thinking is under-utilized in education by both teachers and their students, a problem that cognitive tools may help to ameliorate.

Effects of Learning with and of Technology

Salomon, Perkins, and Globerson make an important distinction between the effects of learning with and of technology:

> "First, we distinguish between two kinds of cognitive effects: Effects with technology obtained during intellectual partnership with it, and the effects of it in terms of the transferable cognitive residue that this partnership leaves behind in the form of better mastery of skills and strategies."

Cognitive tools are important in both respects. Salomon et al. maintain that "the cognitive effects with computer tools greatly depend on the mindful engagement of learners in the tasks afforded by these tools", and that educators should empower learners with cognitive tools and assess their abilities in conjunction with the use of these tools.

Such a development will entail a new conception of ability as an intellectual partnership between learners and the tools they use.

Although some worry that this partnership makes learners too dependent upon the technology, many performances (e.g., instrumental music) are meaningless without the technologies which enable them. Allowing students to demonstrate learning in collaboration with cognitive tools may be attacked by parties invested in existing assessment systems. However, who would assess the ability of an artist without allowing the use of brushes, paint, and other media?

Contemporary intellectual abilities should not be assessed without cognitive tools, including books and computers. The very conception of knowledge is changing with a move from a conception of knowledge as possession of facts and figures to one of knowledge as the ability to retrieve information from databases and use it to solve problems. Of course, there are many important intellectual abilities that should be performed and assessed without the aid of cognitive tools. This is where Salomon et al.'s delineation of the learning effects of technology become so important:

Until intelligent technologies become as ubiquitous as pencil and paper - and we are not there yet by a long shot - how a person functions away from intelligent technologies must be considered. Moreover, even if computer technology became as ubiquitous as the pencil, students will still face an infinite number of problems to solve, new kinds of knowledge to mentally construct, and decisions to make, for which no intelligent technology would be available or accessible.

Many instructional innovations falsely promise to make learning fun and teaching easy. Cognitive tools make no such promises, either for learners or teachers. Instead, cognitive tools activate complex cognitive learning strategies and critical thinking. These tools not only extend the mind, they have the potential to reorganize mental functioning and engage learners in high level generative information processing.

In generative processing, deeper information processing results from activating appropriate mental models, using them to interpret new information, assimilating new information back into those models, reorganizing the models in light of the newly interpreted information, and using the enhanced mental models to explain, interpret, or infer new knowledge. Knowledge acquisition and integration is a constructive process involving "mindful" cognitive effort. When using cognitive tools, learners engage in knowledge construction rather than knowledge reproduction.

Cognitive tools are learner-controlled, not teacher-controlled or technology-driven. For example, when students build databases, they are also constructing their own conceptualization of the organization of a domain of knowledge.

Cognitive tools are not designed to reduce information processing, that is, make a task easier, as has long been the goal of instructional systems design as a field. Learners can't use cognitive tools effortlessly because they require learners to think harder about the subject matter being studied or the task being undertaken with the goal of generating original thoughts that would be impossible without these tools.

The nature and source of the task or problem is paramount in applications of cognitive tools. Past failures of "tool" approaches to using computers in education can be attributed largely to the relegation of the tools to traditional academic tasks set by teachers or the curriculum.

Cognitive tools are intended to be used by students to represent knowledge and solve problems while pursuing investigations that are relevant to their own lives. These investigations are ideally situated within a constructivist learning environment. Cognitive tools won't be effective when used to support teacher-controlled tasks alone.

Foundations for Using Cognitive Tools

The following principles sum up the foundations for using cognitive tools:

- Cognitive tools will have their greatest effectiveness when they are applied within constructivist learning environments.
- Cognitive tools empower learners to design their own representations of knowledge rather than absorbing representations preconceived by others.
- Cognitive tools can be used to support the deep reflective thinking that is necessary for meaningful learning.
- Cognitive tools have two kinds of important cognitive effects, those which are with the technology in terms of intellectual partnerships and those that are of the technology in terms of the cognitive residue that remains after the tools are used.

— Cognitive tools enable mindful, challenging learning rather than the effortless learning promised but rarely realized by other instructional innovations.

— The source of the tasks or problems to which cognitive tools are applied should be learners, guided by teachers and other resources in the learning environment.

— Ideally, tasks or problems for the application of cognitive tools will be situated in realistic contexts with results that are personally meaningful for learners.

Multimedia as a Cognitive Tool

Although there are many different types of computer-based cognitive tools, including databases, spreadsheets, semantic networks, expert systems, multimedia/hypermedia construction software, computer-based conferencing, collaborative knowledge construction environments, computer programming languages, microworlds, and interactive learning environments, multimedia construction software programs such as HyperStudio are tools increasingly available in K-12 schools, and therefore deserve special attention.

Multimedia is the integration of more than one medium into some form of communication or experience delivered via a computer. Most often, multimedia refers to the integration of media such as text, sound, graphics, animation, video, imaging, and spatial modeling into a computer system.

Employing relatively inexpensive desktop computers, users are now able to capture sounds and video, manipulate audio and images to achieve special effects, synthesize audio and video, create sophisticated graphics including animation, and integrate them all into a single multimedia presentation.

Individuals with very little experience are becoming their own multimedia artists, producers, and publishers. Multimedia presentations are engaging because they are multimodal. In other words, multimedia can stimulate more than one sense at a time, and in doing so, may be more attention-getting and attention-holding.In the cognitive tools approach, multimedia is not a form of instruction to learn from, but rather a tool for constructing and learning with. Learners may create their own multimedia knowledge representations that reflect their own perspectives on or understanding of ideas. Or learners may collaborate with other learners to develop a classroom or school multimedia knowledge base.

Ideally, tasks or problems for the application of multimedia construction software as a cognitive tool should be situated in realistic contexts with results that are personally meaningful for learners. Beichner reports on a project where these conditions were met in a unique way. The subjects in this study were seventh and eight grade students enrolled in a middle school located on the grounds of a large, metropolitan zoo. The school is a magnet school emphasizing the study of science to which students are admitted based upon a lottery. A primarily qualitative, observational investigation was conducted over a two-year period while the students worked cooperatively to create interactive displays for a touch-sensitive multimedia kiosk for the zoo.

Several categories emerged out of the qualitative analysis of the data which included extensive videotapes, interviews, observations, and student-created materials. The students' strong appreciation that they were preparing multimedia materials for a real audience emerged as the core category in the analysis. Related findings were:

1) students demonstrated great concern for accuracy in their displays,
2) students quickly assumed the major responsibility for content and editing decisions despite the fact that the original task of designing the displays had been structured for them by the teacher,
3) students accessed wide ranges of science materials and sources to find the content they desired, and
4) their commitment to and enthusiasm for the project remained very high.

On the negative side, the project failed to integrate its activities into the larger curriculum in the school or to attract the participation of teachers other than the computer coordinator. The bottom line was that by establishing an environment where creative thinking about content is combined with real-world assignments, students learned the content, enjoyed the learning process, and recognized that they had created something worthwhile. Lehrer describes the development, use, and results of a hypermedia/ multimedia construction tool called HyperAuthor that was used by eighth graders to design their own lessons about the American Civil War. This study exemplifies the principle that: "Cognitive tools empower learners to design their own representations of knowledge rather than absorbing knowledge representations preconceived by others."

Knowledge is a process of design and not something to be transmitted from teacher to student. Thus, students should be engaged in "HyperComposition" by designing their own hypermedia. The process requires learners to transform information into dimensional representations, determine what is important and what is not, segment information into nodes, link the information segments by semantic relationships, and decide how to represent ideas. This is a highly motivating process because authorship results in ownership of the ideas in the multimedia presentation.

Students in the Lehrer study were high and low ability eighth graders who worked at the multimedia construction tasks for one class period of 45 minutes each day over a period of several months. The students worked in the school media center where they had access to a color Macintosh computer, scanner, sound digitizer, HyperAuthor software, and numerous print and non-print resources about the American Civil War.

An instructor was also available to coach students in the conceptualization, design, and production of the hypermedia programs. Students created programs reflecting their unique interests and individual differences. For example, they created programs about the role of women in the American Civil War, the perspectives of slaves toward the war, and "not-so-famous people" from that period.

According to Lehrer, "The most striking finding was the degree of student involvement and engagement". Both high and low ability students became very task-oriented, increasingly so as they gained more autonomy and confidence with the cognitive tools. At the end of the study, students in the hypermedia group and a control group of students who had studied the Civil War via traditional classroom methods during the same period of time were given an identical teacher-constructed test of knowledge. No significant test differences were found. Lehrer conjectured that "these measures were not valid indicators of the extent of learning in the hypermedia design groups, perhaps because much of what students developed in the design context was not anticipated by the classroom teacher".

However, a year later, when students in the design and control groups were interviewed by an independent interviewer unconnected with the previous year's work, important differences were found. Students in the control group could recall almost nothing about the historical content, whereas students in the design group displayed elaborate concepts and ideas that they had extended to other areas of history.

Most importantly, although students in the control group defined history as "the record of the facts of the past," students in the design class defined history as "a process of interpreting the past from different perspectives." In short, the "design approach lead to knowledge that was richer, better connected, and more applicable to subsequent learning and events".

Lehrer, Erickson, and Connell conducted another study with ninth grade students who were using HyperAuthor to develop hypermedia about topics such as World War I, lifestyles between 1870 and 1920, immigration, and imperialism. They found similar results to the aforementioned Civil War project:

1) students' on-task behavior increased over time,

2) students perceived the benefits of planning and transforming stages of development, and

3) they developed generalizable skills such as taking notes, finding information, coordinating their work with other team members, writing interpretations, and designing presentations.

The Highly Interactive Computing Environments (HI-CE) Group at the University of Michigan has developed a multimedia composition tool called MediaText. They believe that rather than using media to deliver instruction to learners, learners should use the media to generate their own instruction, and in so doing, learn more about the content. The HI-CE group has studied high school students creating MediaText stories, biographies, or instructional aids, as well as multimedia essays.

Students have learned to use techniques such as mentioning, directives, titling, and juxtaposition in their documents. They have found that as students' experiences with MediaText increase, their documents become more integrated rather than merely annotated text. Students have been very enthusiastic about being "constructionists", believing that they are learning more because they understand the ideas better.

The ACCESS (American Culture in Context: Enrichment for Secondary Schools) Project focuses on the subjects commonly taught in high school, such as United States History, American Literature, and American Studies. The project began with teachers assembling a collection of textual, pictorial, audio, and video materials to supplement their courses.

Initially, students simply used the materials for information retrieval. Students who made more extensive use of the conceptual organization built into the system benefited more than the students who used the system like a linear electronic book. Eventually, the project orientation shifted from teacher-created hypermedia materials to student-generated hypermedia documents.

To make it easier for students to create interactive projects, the ACCESS user interface was improved. Students produce several small hypermedia documents of increasing size and complexity early in the school year to become familiar with the authoring process. Later, they generally take on one or more major research projects.

According to Spoehr, the structures that students impose on their hypermedia knowledge vary. A few students (5 - 10%) typically underutilize the power of the programs and use a linear format (i.e., one overview card followed by a linear series of screens). Most students produce more interesting organizational types, including the "star" in which the entry point is an overview containing buttons to two or more sub-topics, each of which appears as a linear sequence, and the "tree" in which one or more main branches off the initial overview in the program are subdivided into further sub-topics which are then organized as linear sequences or divided into sub-sub-topics. Students utilizing the "tree" organization (about 25% of the students) generally show more sophisticated understanding of the topic than students using the "star" structure.

There are many ways that the ACCESS Project students appear to benefit from their experiences as interactive authors, most of which fall into the category of superior knowledge representation and higher-order thinking skills. Spoehr reports that students who build and use hypermedia apparently develop a proficiency in organizing knowledge about a subject in a more expert-like fashion. They are able to represent multiple linkages between ideas and organize concepts into meaningful clusters. In turn, these superior knowledge representations support more complex arguments in written essays. These studies indicate that the conceptual organization skills acquired through building hypermedia/multimedia are sufficiently robust to allow students to generalize these skills to content that they acquire from other sources.

The studies reviewed above support the conclusion that designing multimedia is a complex process that engages many skills in learners. Carver, Lehrer, Connell, and Ericksen list some of the major thinking skills that learners learn and use as multimedia designers:

1. Project Management Skills
   - — Creating a timeline for the completion of the project.
   - — Allocating resources and time to different parts of the project.
   - — Assigning roles to team members.
2. Research Skills
   - — Determining the nature of the problem and how research should be organized.
   - — Posing thoughtful questions about structure, models, cases, values, and roles.
   - — Searching for information using text, electronic, and pictorial information sources.
   - — Developing new information with interviews, questionnaires and other survey methods.
   - — Analyzing and interpreting all the information collected to identify and interpret patterns.

3. Organization and Representation Skills

   — Deciding how to segment and sequence information to make it understandable.

   — Deciding how information will be represented (text, pictures, movies, audio, etc.).

   — Deciding how the information will be organized (hierarchy, sequence) and how it will be linked.

4. Presentation Skills

   — Mapping the design onto the presentation and implementing the ideas in multimedia.

   — Attracting and maintaining the interests of the intended audiences.

5. Reflection Skills

   — Evaluating the program and the process used to create it.

   — Revising the design of the program using feedback.

A search of the ERIC database indicates that there were at least 250 publications related to the use of multimedia in schools in 1997. But perusal of these articles indicates that the vast majority are based upon the perception that multimedia is something that students learn "from" rather than "with." There are very few schools where multimedia construction software is consistently used as cognitive tools, and even fewer research and evaluation studies of the type described above.

Research focused on multimedia seems to be stuck in the traditional comparative paradigm. To give but one example, White and Kuhn compared elementary school students' ability to recall stories about historical figures presented to them via text, oral reading, and multimedia presentations. No significant differences were found, a finding typical of the last 50 years of media comparison research. A more fruitful investigation might have examined the effects of having students create their own multimedia representations of stories. Ironically, while using multimedia as a cognitive tool remains on the fringe of mainstream K-12 education, most school systems are rushing to hook themselves up to the Internet to provide teachers and students with access to multimedia information on the World Wide Web.

Constructivist Learning Environments

A constructivist learning environment is a place where learners may work together and support each other as they use a variety of tools and information resources in their guided pursuit of learning goals and problem-solving activities. For the cognitive scientists, learning theorists, instructional designers, and teachers involved in creating constructivist learning environments, learning refers to the development of mental states and abilities of all types including conceptual knowledge, technical skills, automatic rules, mental models, and problem-solving.

Forms of higher-order outcomes such as motivation, intellectual curiosity, and the habits of lifelong learning are especially relevant because these are the most challenging types of learning to teach and learn. According to Honebein, to meet these ambitious learning outcomes, developers of constructivist learning environments adhere to seven goals:

1. Provide students with experience with the knowledge construction process.
2. Provide experience in and appreciation for multiple perspectives.

3. Embed learning in realistic and relevant contexts.
4. Encourage ownership and voice in the learning process.
5. Embed learning in social experience.
6. Encourage the use of multiple modes of representation.
7. Encourage self-awareness of the knowledge construction process.

The research findings associated with different types of constructivist learning environments, specifically, a microworld called LEGO/Logo, a classroom-based learning environment called Jasper Woodbury, and an open, virtual environment called CoVis are described in the following paragraphs:

LEGO/Logo: Logo was created by Seymour Papert. Early investigations of Logo as a programming language that would enable students to develop generalizable problem-solving skills were not as successful as Papert and others predicted. More recently, new versions of Logo have been developed that involve real objects that children can program with Logo instructions. The best known of these is LEGO/Logo, which integrates a popular building block toy set with computer-controlled devices such as motors. With two to four students per group, children in grades 3-5 tackle design problems such as creating a LEGO walking machine. In addition to physical tasks (building robots) and mental tasks (programming actions), the students keep "Inventors Notebooks."

Early qualitative studies of children engaging in the LEGO/Logo projects yielded positive results. Resnick and Ocko summarize the results:

> Our work has shown that Constructionist design activities offer rich learning opportunities. Far from obscuring mathematical and scientific concepts, design projects can actually give mathematical and scientific concepts a new relevance in the minds of children. Moreover, such projects can provide students with a new appreciation of how real mathematicians and scientists (not to mention architects and engineers and writers) go about their work.

An extension of the LEGO/Logo work has led to the development of a "programmable brick" and other objects that students can use in constructionist design projects. Research continues at the M.I.T. Media Lab and local schools in the Boston area to test these and other microworlds.

Jasper Woodbury: The Cognition and Technology Group at Vanderbilt University is well known for the development of a rich set of classroom-based learning environments that address a wide range of curriculum goals including mathematics and problem-solving. The most heavily researched versions of these programs are known as the Jasper Woodbury Problem-Solving Series.

Available in both linear video and interactive videodisc formats, these programs are based around interesting vignettes that present middle school-age students with challenging problems to solve. For example, in one episode, a hiker finds a wounded eagle in a remote mountain site that can only be reached by personal aircraft. The students must figure out the best route to fly while dealing with variables such as wind conditions and fuel capacity. Students work in small teams to solve these problems. There are multiple possible solutions, and conditions such as wind speed can be changed to create analog and extension problems.

A year-long research project was conducted with Jasper in 16 schools in 9 states. Comparing students in Jasper classes with those in traditional math classes, the researchers investigated effects in terms of mathematical problem-solving and reasoning skills, specific mathematical knowledge and skills, standardized achievement test scores, and attitudes toward mathematics. The study used both quantitative and qualitative methods.

The results were generally favorable for the Jasper students. With respect to problem-solving, the Jasper students were more skilled in identifying problems and breaking them down into smaller components that would lead to solutions. Regarding specific knowledge and skills, the Jasper students outperformed the control students in areas such as decimals, fractions, and calculations of area, perimeter, and volume. The Jasper students also were better in solving three different types of word problems. Results were less positive in the attitude and achievement areas.

Although the Jasper students had more positive attitudes toward mathematics at the end of the school year, they expressed no greater desire to study math than the control students. On standardized achievement tests, Jasper students tended to perform better than the others, but the results were not statistically significant.

A more recent study investigated the effects of immersing fifth grade students in Jasper Adventures for three months. The results were equally positive, with the Jasper students outperforming the control students in mathematical and scientific knowledge, higher level problem-solving skills, learning skills, and even creativity.

The CoVis Project: With funding from the National Science Foundation (NSF) in the USA, researchers at

Northwestern University have been developing the "CoVis Collaboratory," a learning environment that combines the objects and tools of constructivism with communication and visualization tools that enable communication and collaboration among learners in a sociocultural context. Working in 40 high school science classrooms, CoVis has three key components:

1. project-based science learning pedagogy,
2. scientific visualization tools for open-ended inquiry, and
3. networked environments for synchronous and asynchronous communication and collaboration.

Projects can be designed in a variety of scientific disciplines. Some of the most interesting involve atmospheric sciences examining issues such as "global warming." CoVis is currently undergoing extensive research and evaluation, and early results indicate that students spend their time productively, prefer CoVis activities over traditional science labs, and learn both content and scientific inquiry skills. Additional research is focusing on teachers' roles in the Collaboratory.

Up until now, most research focused on forms of computer-based learning systems has investigated how to use the limited capabilities of the computer to present information and judge learner input (neither of which computers do especially well) while asking learners to memorize information and later recall it on tests (which computers do with far greater speed and accuracy than humans).

The cognitive tools and constructivist learning environment approaches described above assign cognitive responsibility to each part of the learning system that does it best. The learner is responsible for recognizing and judging patterns of information, organizing it, and representing knowledge, while the computer performs calculations, stores information, and retrieves it upon the learner's command.

Nonetheless, helping people to change their mental models of computers as something that students learn "from" to something they learn "with" remains a great challenge. This probably has a great deal to do with the constructivist pedagogy that ideally guides the adaptation of cognitive tools in schools. Many teachers are uncomfortable with moving from a teacher-centered to student-centered classroom environment, and such a transformation takes considerable time and support.

Design of Media and Technology for Education

Media and technology can be more or less well-designed depending on the talents, resources, and timelines available for the development effort. There are numerous scientific principles to guide design, but every instructional development effort involves large amounts of creativity and hard work. There are no comprehensive or infallible instructional design formulas. In fact, the design of media and technology for education retains as many aspects of a craft as it does a science. Evaluation has an especially important role in the instructional design process, but it is often underutilized.

Implementation at the local level is as important as instructional design. In most instances, the conditions under which students actually experience and use media and technology in schools are decided within the confines of single classrooms by individual teachers. While some educational technologists have recommended that media and technology innovations should be "teacher-proof" to ensure fidelity in implementation, teacher empowerment is more likely to have positive effects than attempts to limit the prerogatives of teachers to implement media and technology as they wish.

The Apple Classroom of Tomorrow (ACOT) Project illustrates the enormous importance of implementation in efforts to infuse media and technology into classrooms. In 1985, Apple Computer, Inc. began a long-term collaboration with several widely-separated school districts around the USA. Students and teachers were provided with computers and software for both school and home use, and research has been conducted in the participating schools for over a decade. The ambitious research program focused on six major questions:

1. What kinds of collaborative environments and tools are most helpful in inquiry-based classrooms?
2. What happens when teachers and students have access to rich on-line resources and remote experts?
3. How can the computer's power to represent knowledge in multiple media support learning?
4. How can the computer be used to support students in problem-solving?
5. What happens to motivation and learning when students have the same access to the sophisticated tools that experts use?
6. How can the learning and competencies accomplished in a technology-rich environment be assessed?

Coley et al. summarize the results of the first decade of ACOT research:

ACOT students:

— Explored and represented information dynamically and in many forms
— Became socially aware and more confident
— Communicated effectively about complex processes
— Used technology routinely and appropriately
— Became independent learners and self-starters knew their areas of expertise and shared that expertise spontaneously
— Worked well collaboratively
— Developed a positive orientation to the future.

Some of the most interesting findings from the ACOT research concern teachers and implementation. ACOT researchers found that teachers had strong beliefs about their roles and efficacy as teachers which changed very slowly as their classrooms moved toward child-centered rather than textbook-driven education.

Teachers had to make significant changes in their classroom management styles, giving up more control to technology and students. This also changed slowly. Initially, media and technology were primarily used within the context of traditional pedagogical methods, and most teachers required years of experience before they adopted more innovative strategies such as project-based learning. Finally, teachers struggled with fundamental incongruities between traditional assessment measures and the kinds of learning occurring in their classrooms. In fact, assessment problems proved to be the most resistant to solutions and many remained unresolved.

The bottom line of the ACOT Project is that pedagogical innovations and positive learning results do eventually emerge from the infusion of media and technology into schools, but the process takes longer than most people imagine. Educational administrators who imagine that a summer workshop or after-school seminars by consultants will enable teachers to implement media and technology in their classrooms are mistaken. Huge investments in time and support for teachers will be especially critical if the adoption of constructivist pedagogies accompany the infusion of media and technology.

3

Children and Media Violence

Compared to previous years, today's are becoming more and more violent in their day-to-day life. They are becoming so self-centred all are willing to do any illegal activities for their own puropse. For example, in United States, the law enforcement agencies arrested an estimated 2.8 millions persons under age 18.1 in 1997. Of that number, an estimated 2,500 juveniles were arrested for murder and 121,000 for other violent crimes. According to the Federal Bearou of Investigation (FBI), juveniles accounted for 19% of all arrests, 14% of all murder arrests, and 17% of all violent crime arrests in 1997. While the number of arrests of juveniles for violent crimes declined slightly from 1996 to 1997, the number of juvenile violent crime arrests in 1997 was still 49% above the 1988 level.

James Q. Wilson, one of the foremost experts on crime, has observed, "Youngsters are shooting at people at a far higher rate than at any time in recent history." The Centers for Disease Control and Prevention (CDC) reports that a recent survey showed that some 5.9% of the American high school students surveyed said that they had carried a gun in the 30 days prior to the survey. Equally troubling, that survey also shows that 18% of high school students now carry a knife, razor, firearm, or other weapon on a regular basis, and 9% of them take a weapon to school. While recent studies show that the amount of youth violence has started to decline, the CDC warns that "the prevalence of youth violence and school violence is still unacceptably high."

As a result of demographic trends, the problem of juvenile violence could dramatically worsen as the number of American teenagers will increase significantly over the next decade. According to Department of Justice estimates, the number of juveniles who will be arrested for violent crimes will double by the year 2010.

Countless studies have shown that a steady diet of television, movie, music, video game, and Internet violence plays a significant role in the disheartening number of violent acts committed by youth.

Impact of TV and Cinema Violence

With respect to television violence alone, a 1993 report by University of Washington epidemiologist Brandon S. Centerwall expresses a startling finding: "[If], hypothetically, television technology had never been developed, there would be 10,000 fewer homicides each year in the United States, 70,000 fewer rapes, and 700,000 fewer injurious assaults. Violent crime would be half what it is." Plainly, any solution to the juvenile violence problem that fails to address media violence is doomed to failure.

American media are exceedingly violent. With television, analysis of programming for 20 years found that over the years, the level of violence in prime-time programming remained at about 5 violent acts per hour. An August 1994 report by the Center for Media and Public Affairs reported that in one 18-hour day in 1992, observing 10 channels of all major kinds of programs, 1,846 different scenes of violence were noted, which translated to more than 10 violent scenes per hour, per channel, all day. A follow-up study conducted in 1994, found a 41% increase in violent scenes to 2,605, which translated to almost 15 scenes of violence per hour.

Like television, the cinemas are full of movies that glamorize bloodshed and violence, and one need only listen to popular music radio and stroll down the aisle of almost any computer store to see that the music and video games are similarly afflicted.

Not only are the media exceedingly violent; they are also ubiquitous. The percentage of households with more than one television set has reached an all-time high of 87%, and roughly ½ of American children have a television set in their room. Forty-six percent of all homes with children have access to at least one television set, a VCR, home video game equipment and a personal computer, and 88.7% of such homes have either home video game equipment, a personal computer, or both.

Most children now have unprecedented technological avenues for accessing the "entertainment" the media industries provide. In USA, the average 7th grader watches about 4 hours of television per day, and 60% of those shows contain some violence. The average 7th grader plays electronic games at least 4 hours per week, and 50% of those games are violent.

According to the American Psychiatric Association, by age 18 an American child will have seen 16,000 simulated murders and 200,000 acts of violence. The

Littleton, Colorado school massacre has spawned a national debate over how to respond to this culture of media violence. In May 1999, a USA Today/CNN/Gallup poll found that 73% of Americans believe that TV and movies are partly to blame for juvenile crime. A TIME/CNN poll found that 75% of teens 13 to 17 years of age believe the Internet is partly responsible for crimes like the Littleton shootings, 66% blame violence in movies, television, and music, and 56% blame video game violence.

More than 1,000 studies on the effects of television and film violence have been done during the past 40 years. In the last decade the American Medical Association, the American Academy of Pediatrics, the American Academy of Child and Adolescent Psychiatry, and the National Institute of Mental Health have separately reviewed many of these studies. Each of these reviews has reached the same conclusion: television violence leads to real-world violence. The National Institute of Mental Health reported that "television violence is as strongly correlated with aggressive behavior as any variable that has been measured."

A comprehensive study conducted by the Surgeon General's Office in 1972, and updated in 1982, found television violence a contributing factor to increases in violent crime and antisocial behavior; a 1984 United States Attorney General's Task Force study on family violence revealed that viewing television violence contributed to acting-out violence in the home; and recently, the National Television Violence Study, a 3-year project that examined the depiction of violent behavior across more than 8,200 programs, concluded that televised violence teaches aggressive attitudes and behaviors, desensitization to violence, and increased fear of becoming victimized by violence. The majority of the existing social and behavioral science studies, taken together, agree on the following basic points:

(1) constant viewing of televised violence has negative effects on human character and attitudes;

(2) television violence encourages violent forms of behavior and influences moral and social values about violence in daily life;

(3) children who watch significant amounts of television violence have a greater likelihood of exhibiting later aggressive behavior;

(4) television violence affects viewers of all ages, intellect, socioeconomic levels, and both genders; and

(5) viewers who watch significant amounts of television violence perceive a meaner world and overestimate the possibility of being a victim of violence.

The research has also shown that television violence can harm even young children. Researchers have performed longitudinal studies of the impact of television violence on young children as they mature into adults. One such study, begun in 1960, examined 600 people at age 8, age 18, and age 30. The researchers concluded that boys at age 8 who had been watching more television violence than other boys grew up to be more aggressive than other boys, and they also grew up to be more aggressive and violent than one would have expected them to be on the basis of how aggressive they were as 8-year-olds.

A second similar study, which included girls, arrived at a similar conclusion: children who watched more violence behaved more aggressively the next year than those who watched less violence on television, and more aggressively than anticipated based on their behavior the previous year. Professor L. Rowell Huesmann, one of the researchers behind these studies, summarized his findings before a Senate committee earlier this year:

> Not every child who watches a lot of violence or plays a lot of violent games will grow up to be violent. Other forces must converge, as they did recently in Colorado. But just as every cigarette increases the chance that someday you will get lung cancer, every exposure to violence increases the chances that some day a child will behave more violently than they otherwise would.

Some experts also believe that children can become addicted to violence. "Violence is like the nicotine in cigarettes," states Lt. Col. Dave Grossman, a former Green Beret and West Point psychology professor who now heads the Killology Research Group. "The reason why the media has to pump ever more violence into us is because we've built up a tolerance. In order to get the same high, we need ever-higher levels. . . . The television industry has gained its market share through an addictive and toxic ingredient."

The American Academy of Pediatrics recently published a report advocating a national media education program to mitigate the negative impact of the harmful media messages seen and heard by children and adolescents. Robert Lichter, president of the Center for Media and Public Affairs, a nonprofit research group in Washington, D.C., has framed the issue in language we can all understand: "If you're worried about what your kid eats, you should worry about what your kid's watching."

Less research has been done on the effect of music, video games, and the Internet on children. Nonetheless, on the basis of both that research and the research findings concerning television and film, experts confidently predict that violent music, video games, and Internet material also will be found to have harmful effects on children.

Impact of Songs with Violent Lyrics

In Plato's Republic, Socrates said that "musical training is a more potent instrument than any other, because rhythm and harmony find their way into the inward places of the soul, on which they mightily fasten." Music affects our moods, our attitudes, our emotions, and our behavior; we wake to it, dance to it, and sometimes cry to it. From infancy it is an integral part of our lives. As virtually any parent with a teenager can attest, music holds an even more special place in the hearts and minds of our young people. Academic studies confirm this wisdom.

One survey of 2,760 14-to-16-year-olds in 10 different cities found that they listened to music an average of 40 hours per week. Research has also shown that the average teenager listens to 10,500 hours of rock music during the years between the 7th and 12th grades. Inadequate attention has been paid to the effect on children of violent music lyrics. Although no studies have documented a cause-and-effect relationship between violent lyrics and aggressive behavior, studies do indicate that a preference for heavy metal music may be a significant marker for alienation, substance abuse, psychiatric disorders, suicide risk, sex-role stereotyping, or risk-taking behaviors during adolescence.

A Swedish study has found that adolescents who developed an early interest in rock music were more likely to be influenced by their peers and less influenced by their parents than older adolescents. With good reason, then, parents are concerned about the music lyrics their children hear. And parents should be concerned. Despite historic, bipartisan remedial legislation by the state and federal governments, it is stunning even to the casual listener how much modern music glorifies acts of violence.

Studies show that modern music lyrics have become increasingly explicit, particularly concerning sex, drugs, and, most troubling, violence against women. For example, the rock band Nine Inch Nails released a song titled "Big Man with a Gun," which triumphantly describes a sexual assault at gun point. Such hatred and violence against women are widespread and unmistakable in mainstream hip-hop and alternative music. Consider the singer "Marilyn Manson," whose less vulgar lyrics include: "Who says date rape isn't kind?"; "Let's just kill everyone and let your god sort them out"; and "The housewife I will beat, the pro-life I will kill." Other Manson lyrics cannot be repeated here. Or consider "Eminem," the hip-hop artist featured frequently on MTV, who recently wrote "Bonnie and Clyde," a song in which he described killing his child's mother and dumping her body in the ocean.

One should hope that the music industry would, at the very least, ostracize such material. Regrettably, however, the industry has chosen to embrace it. How else would the industry explain a 1998 Grammy nomination for Nine Inch Nails? A 1999 Grammy nomination for Marilyn Manson? MTV's "Best New Artist" award to Marilyn Manson last year and Eminem this year? Or the fact that, despite growing concern about such music, Eminem and Nine Inch Nails performed just last week at MTV's Video Music Awards show, televised across the country during prime time? It would be inconsistent with the First Amendment freedoms for government to prohibit such music. But surely it is not too much to ask that the music industry refrain from rewarding and celebrating these purveyors of filth and violence. It must not be ignored that these violent, misogynist images may ultimately affect the behavior and attitudes of many young men toward women. Writing about such lyrics in 1996, William J. Bennett, Senator Joseph Lieberman, and C. DeLores Tucker posed the following question: "What would you do if you discovered that someone was encouraging your sons to kill people indiscriminately, to find fun in beating and raping girls, and to use the word 'motherf-er' at least once in every sentence?"

Many people are concerned with potential deleterious effects of listening to songs with violent lyrics. An accumulating body of scientific research spanning 4 decades supports the hypothesis that exposure to violent media is causally related to subsequent expression of aggression in both short- and long-term time frames. The vast majority of this research has focused on violent television and movies. Recently, a small but relatively consistent research literature has shown that short-term exposure to violent video games causes increases in aggression and aggression-related variables. Nonetheless, there remains among the general population and many practitioners a very strong belief in the age-old *catharsis hypothesis*—the belief that experiencing and expressing aggressive emotions and thoughts will decrease subsequent aggressive thoughts, feelings, and emotions. This ancient Greek idea, later popularized by Breuer and Freud and now usually labeled *venting*, states that aggressive impulses can be reduced by watching, reading, or singing about anger and aggression as well as by behaving in symbolically aggressive ways. Though the aggression catharsis hypothesis has been thoroughly explored and debunked in several entertainment media domains, there has been relatively little work on the effects of songs with violent lyrics on aggression-related variables such as aggressive thoughts and feelings.

There are numerous differences between watching violent television, playing violent video games, and listening to popular music. One is the lack of a video component to audio-only music. Another is that aggressive lyrical content of popular music is often discernible only to the most attentive of listeners, whereas videobased media (including music videos) make their violent content abundantly and graphically clear. Some rock music songs have such garbled lyrics that they have given rise to debates about what the lyrics are. A third difference concerns attention. A large proportion of time spent listening to music involves paying attention to the music (not the lyrics) or to other tasks. Thus, effects of violent lyrics may generally be attenuated (relative to video-based media violence) simply because the lyrics are not processed by the listeners.

Nonetheless, there are valid reasons to worry about potentially harmful effects of violent music lyrics. Numerous studies have shown that aggressive words can prime aggressive thoughts, perceptions, and behavior. Indeed, such effects can occur even when the stimulus has not been consciously recognized. Furthermore, listeners are capable of recognizing themes of music (i.e., violence, sex, suicide, and Satanism) even when it is difficult to comprehend specific lyric content. Additionally, music stimuli are played repeatedly, both by radio stations as well as by listeners themselves. Another difference between video-based entertainment and music concerns the amount of imagination needed or allowed to fill in details of the story being told. The lack of visual images in music both allows and requires listeners to imagine details. Concrete images probably play a major role in transfer of ideas from the video world to one's own real-world situations. When one's video antagonists are similar to one's real antagonists, violent solutions modeled in the video world are more likely to be attempted in the real world than when the video antagonists are dissimilar. The lack of concrete images in violent music may well allow listeners to imagine audio antagonists similar to real-world antagonists. Thus, there are reasons to expect violent-lyric songs to be either more or less influential than violent video materials.

Several field and laboratory experiments have examined effects of aggressive music videos. Waite, Hillbrand, and Foster observed a significant decrease in aggressive behavior on a forensic inpatient ward after removal of Music Television (MTV). Peterson and Pfost found that exposing males to nonerotic violent music videos led to a significant increase in adversarial sexual beliefs and negative affect. Johnson, Jackson, and Gatto found that males who had been randomly assigned to view violent rap music videos became more accepting of the use of violence in dealing with interpersonal problems. Related research found that males and females exposed to violent rap music videos became more accepting of teen dating violence. College students exposed to rock music videos with antisocial themes produced a greater acceptance of antisocial behavior. Students were also more likely to accept stereotypic sex-role behavior after being exposed to music videos that displayed similar behavior.

Music video studies are valuable in their own right, but they do not provide information about the effects of exposure to violent lyrics without video. Music videos are much more like other video media (TV, movies) in that they can tell a story with graphically violent images; the finding that they produce similar effects is not surprising.

Correlational studies have suggested a connection between the kind of music youth listen to and various maladaptive behaviors and attitudes, though the direction of causality is not clear. Rubin, West, and Mitchell found that college students who preferred rap and heavy metal music reported more hostile attitudes than students who preferred other genres of music, such as alternative, adult contemporary, dance–soul, or country. Listeners to heavy metal music held more negative attitudes toward women. Rap music fans were more distrustful.

Similarly, Took and Weiss found a correlation between preference for rap and heavy metal music and below-average academic performance, school behavior problems, drug use, arrests, and sexual activity. Still other studies have found correlations between music type preferences and a variety of maladaptive behaviors but have not specifically linked lyric preferences to those behaviors.

McFarland looked at the effects of exposure to tense, calm, or no-background music (without lyrics) on the emotional content of stories written for the Thematic Apperception Test. Participants who heard tense music wrote the most unpleasant stories. Like the music video studies, these results tell us little about lyric effects. However, they indicate that research on lyrics must control for effects of type of music.

Only a few studies have specifically examined the influence of violent songs on aggression-related variables. Interestingly, most have found no effects of lyrical content.

For example, participants in Ballard and Coates's study heard one of six songs varying in genre (rap vs. heavy metal) and lyric (homicidal, suicidal, neutral). Lyric content had no impact on mood measures, including anger. In other studies showing no effect, the genre of the songs (heavy metal) made the lyrics nearly incomprehensible, a problem noted by the researchers themselves.

Barongan and Hall reported a study suggesting that antisocial lyrics can affect behavior, but the target behavior was not clearly aggressive; thus, its relevance to our work is unclear. Male college students listened to misogynous or neutral rap music, viewed three vignettes and then chose one of the three vignettes to be shown to a female confederate. Those who had listened to the misogynous music were significantly more likely to choose the assaultive vignette. Wester, Crown, Quatman, and Heesacker reported mixed results. Male undergraduates were exposed to either

(a) sexually violent music and lyrics,

(b) the same music without lyrics,

(c) sexually violent lyrics without music, or

(d) no music or lyrics.

Results yielded no differences in negative attitudes toward women among the four groups. However, participants exposed to violent lyrics viewed their relationships with women as more adversarial. Overall, the few published studies on the effects of exposure to songs with violent lyrics have produced mixed results, perhaps because of methodological problems involving confounds with arousal or lyrics that were indecipherable. We build on prior work by using a social–cognitive theoretical perspective that has emerged from aggression research in several different domains, including media violence.

The theoretical basis for the present experiments comes from our earlier work on GAM. This model draws on empirical and theoretical contributions from several research groups, most notably the social–cognitive work of Bandura, Berkowitz, Crick and Dodge, Geen, Huesmann, and Mischel. Effects of situational (e.g., violent media) and personality (e.g., trait hostility) input variables combine (sometimes interactively) to influence aggressive behavior by influencing the present internal state (cognition, affect, and arousal) and subsequent appraisal and decision processes. These main pathways are linked in Figure 1 by the bold lines with arrows. The dashed lines within the Present Internal State box indicate that these components affect each other. Because of potential arousal effects on other variables, it is important to control induced arousal when examining effects on cognition and affect. The focus of this article is lyric effects on current cognition and affect, so we do not discuss appraisal and action aspects of GAM.

According to GAM, long-term effects accrue via the development of highly accessible knowledge structures and emotional desensitization to violence by well-established social–cognitive learning and systematic desensitization processes. In brief, each media violence episode constitutes a learning trial in which one rehearses aggressive thoughts and primes aggression-related affects, creating and making chronically accessible hostile attitudes, beliefs, expectations, and scripts.

Impact of Video Games and Internet

Interactive video games and the Internet have become the entertainment of choice for America's adolescents. Nearly seven in ten homes with children now have a personal computer (68.2%), and 41% of homes with children have access to the Internet. Annual video game revenues in the United States exceed $10 billion, nearly double the amount of money Americans spend going to the movies. On average, American children who have home video game machines play with them about 90 minutes a day.

The video games of choice for the youth are those that contain depictions of violence. A 1993 study, for instance, asked 357 seventh- and eighth-graders to select their preferences among five categories of video games. Thirty-two percent of the children selected the category "fantasy violence," and 17% selected "human violence." Only 2% of the children chose "educational games."

Parents are concerned that the fantasy violence in video games could lead their children to real-world violence. That concern intensified when Americans learned that the two juveniles responsible for the Littleton massacre had obsessively played the ultra-violent video game "Doom." Americans also recalled that the 14-year-old boy who shot eight classmates in Paducah, Kentucky in 1997, had been an avid player of video games. As the New York Times observed, "the search for the cause in the Littleton shootings continues, and much of it has come to focus on violent video games." Here, too, the concern of parents is justified. Studies indicate that violent video games have an effect on children similar to that of violent television and film. That is, prolonged exposure of children to violent video games increases the likelihood of aggression.

Some authorities go even further, concluding that the violent actions performed in playing video games are even more conducive to aggressive behavior. According to this view, the more often children practice fantasy acts of violence, the more likely they are to carry out real-world violent acts. As Professor Brian Stonehill, creator of the media studies program at Pomona College in Claremont, California, states: "The technology is going from passive to active. The violence is no longer vicarious with interactive media. It's much more pernicious and worrisome." Another researcher characterizes such games as sophisticated simulators, similar to those used in military training.

Equally troubling, video games often present violence in a glamorized light. Typical games cast players in the role of a shooter, with points scored for each "kill." Furthermore, advertising for such games often touts the violent conduct as a selling point--the more graphic and extreme, the better. For example, the advertisement for the game "Destrega" reads: "Let the slaughter begin"; and for the game "Subspace," "Meet people from all over the world, then kill them." As the popularity and graphic nature of such games increase, so does the harm to the youth.

4

Media and Child Growth

Child development theory has educated teachers and informed policy makers for 50 years. In the last decade, the same strong foundation of child development principles has been applied to identify the risks of prolonged or inappropriate exposure of children to the media.

The term 'early childhood' generally refers to the years of a child's life from birth to about seven. The central developmental needs in the early childhood years are:

— Developing a sense of trust and safety

— The need for autonomy and connection

— A sense of empowerment and efficacy

— Developing a gender identity

— Understanding how people are alike and different

— Developing a sense of morality and social responsibility

— The need for meaningful play.

Developing a sense of trust and safety: Children need to feel that the world is a safe place and that people can be trusted. This allows them the freedom to explore their world and approach new experience with curiosity and openness.

Appropriate television presents to children a world where people are predictable and can be trusted and where they treat each other with love and kindness.

Many programs present a world filled with violence and evil, where 'bad guys' threaten the safety of 'good guys'. An underlying message of instability and threat is repeated over and over again in many children's programs giving children the impression of a threatening and unsafe world where danger is never put to rest.

Violent and scary television programming is developmentally inappropriate because it undermines children's sense of safety and security. Such programs do not show children how to resolve conflicts non-violently and can heighten children's anxieties about their own safety.

The need for autonomy and connection: It is important for children in the early years to do an increasing range of tasks for themselves. At the same time they also learn to participate more and more in relationships with others.

Developmentally appropriate TV shows children ways to act autonomously while maintaining a positive connection with others. It should present a world where people help and support each other, while maintaining their own independence.

Many cartoons and other children's programs present the themes of separation and connection as if they are mutually exclusive. Autonomy is commonly equated with violence and hurt toward others and connection with helplessness and victimisation.

Television programming that presents its characters as being either autonomous or in relationship don't help children to develop the idea that they can be both independent and connected to others.

A sense of empowerment and efficacy: Children have to develop a sense that they can affect their world and feelings of inner strength and belief in themselves as competent and capable people. To do this, children have to learn exactly what actions, skills and words will have what kinds of effects in different situations.

Appropriate television programs make children feel that they can make a positive difference in the world. It shows a wide range of things that people can do to bring about positive change.

On many children's programs the characters display empowerment and efficacy only by using weapons and violence. Using words and wits to solve problems is not often shown.

Much of current children's television programs undermine development by failing to provide content that helps children develop a sense of empowerment. There are very few characters that serve as role models for achieving positive effects in non-violent ways.

Developing a gender identity: The more broadly children approach the question of what it means to be a 'boy' or a 'girl', the more they are likely to develop to their full potential. Children need to be shown that boys and girls can do a wide range of things, many of which are common to both sexes.

Appropriate television provides models of both sexes engaging in a wide range of activities. Children need to see complex characters who embody characteristics traditionally thought of as both male and female in order to open up possibilities for themselves.

Many of the popular children's shows present a very narrow range of behaviour options to boys and girls. Males are muscle-bound characters who like to fight especially with big weapons. Females are sweet, kind and often sexy, spending a lot of time caring about how they look.

TV can give children a restricted picture of what it means to be a boy or girl, exaggerating a tendency for stereotyping naturally occurring in young children.

Understanding how people are alike and different: Young children are in the process of learning about who they are as individuals and as members of a broader society, about how they are alike an different from other people and about how people of diverse backgrounds and experience treat each other.

Television has the potential to expose children to diverse people and to show them how people can respect and learn from each other. Many children's television programs promote suspicion, intolerance and even violence against those who are different. Racial and ethnic stereotypes are common.

Much of the TV that young children see today impedes their ability to develop an appreciation and respect for differences among people. Few models are presented that show how differences among people can enhance human experience or broaden horizons.

Developing a sense of morality and social responsibility: Young children are developing ideas about morality, justice and how people should treat each other. Children's tendency to divide things up into categories-either all good or all bad, all right or all wrong-makes them particularly susceptible to material presented in simple black-and-white terms.

Television should provide children with many opportunities to learn about being responsible and moral members of a community; they should see people who treat each other with kindness and respect, help one another, and work out problems without resorting to violence.

Most commercial television programs present one-dimensional characters who are either 'all good' or 'all bad', who lack the complexity of real human character. Questions of social responsibility and morality are not raised when good characters attack and maim bad ones.

Much of commercial TV undermines the development of morality and social responsibility. It shows that violence is a justified and even glamorous way to resolve conflict.

The need for meaningful play: Play is basic to the healthy development and learning of children. Through the process of play, children can master experiences that may have been scary or difficult for them, they can learn to think creatively, take risks and solve problems. Children need to be in charge of their own play-they need time, space and props to encourage them.

Role of Television in Child Growth

Television can never substitute for children's direct experiences in interacting with the world. However, it could provide them with the kind of content they need for play. Many themes on commercial television programs are removed from children's experience and understanding. Play becomes merely imitative rather than creative. Single purpose toys marketed along with these shows further the tendency to imitation. Children's television does not help children meet their developmental needs through play. Not only does television cut deeply into play time, it also provides a narrow range of content for children to use in play.

Having a television in a child's bedroom may be a handy way to solve family conflict over who is going to watch what. But it can have its down side. Having the television, or computer game, or Internet access in the child's room means that you can't supervise what your child is watching or playing. You won't know what the TV program, computer game or Internet site is teaching your child. You won't necessarily know if a child has seen something that has disturbed them.

One of the most important roles a parent can play is that of a "media educator". You don't have to be trained teacher to do that. Your comments on programs, your discussions with a child about what they've seen, your expression of your values, your identification of the unrealities of programs and commercials are vital to a child's understanding of what he or she has seen, and the development of critical viewing skills. When the television or computer is in the family room, rather than the bedroom you can make the most of the "teachable moment".

Having the television in the child's bedroom may also allow the child to watch TV right up to bed time. There is good evidence of negative impacts from viewing at bed time. These include bedtime resistance, the delay of the onset of sleep, anxiety which results in shortened sleep duration, night wakings and day time sleepiness. TV, computer games, the Internet are public media. Keep them public, and not in your child's bedroom.

Watching some forms of media content, or watching TV right up to bedtime, can be a contributor to sleep problems and nightmares, especially in young children. Young children are particularly susceptible to being scared by images in films and on TV. Joanne Cantor, author of the most helpful Mommy, I'm scared: How TV and Movies Frighten Children and What We Can Do to Protect Them, has found that children under age eight are especially vulnerable, for the following reasons:

— they have difficulty with fantasy-reality distinction. What they see is real to them.

— they are extremely responsive to visual images, especially those that are graphic, grotesque and gory-even those shown only for a few seconds

— they have relatively little real world sophistication with which they might put what they see in perspective

— they have great difficulty using information provided to them to cast what they are seeing in a different light (i.e. less threatening or something that shouldn't be copied).

Recent research shows that children's anxiety levels have been steadily increasing since the 1950s, and that children's level of anxieties and their frequency of sleep disturbances are significantly related to the amount of television they watch. Children who have been scared by something they've seen on TV may need a lot of reassurance.Watching TV right up to bedtime is not a good idea. Children watching TV or a video have been through an emotional experience, and may need time to "work it off". Time for a bath, reading a story, or a chat with Mum or Dad, will more effectively prepare children for a good night's sleep.

Watching the TV News

When we talk about 'the News', what we are usually talking about is a collection of the worst, and often the most violent, things that have happened in the world on that day. Adults realise that what is on the News does not represent what is likely to happen to them in their daily lives know that the News principally reports on the most violent events from all over the world, often in a sensationalised manner choose to watch the News for a variety of reasons, including that they may wish to be informed about world events, and in the knowledge that many of these events are far removed from their own immediate experience can nonetheless be made to feel depressed and anxious by watching the News.

Children lack grown-ups' experience of the world and so are unable to distinguish between what they see and the likelihood of these events occurring in their own lives may think that when they see the same event over and over again that the event is actually happening over and over again can be made anxious because they think that the events that they see are likely to happen to them. At a young age, they are unable to understand the concept of probability so are not necessarily reassured if you tell them 'it isn't likely to happen to us' may become quite fearful if violence in shown in settings with which they are familiar, such as homes and families, or children and animals.

The risk is greater to primary age children, than to very young children, as older children know that 'the news' is supposed to be the real world and are more likely to identify with the persons and situations in the news. For example they may fear being kidnapped, or that their family might suffer a fate seen in the news particularly catastrophic events such as September 11 in New York pose acute problems for children, as viewing adults' fears will be communicated to the watching children.

It's best to turn off the TV news when your children are in the room. While children should not be shielded from the realities of the world, 'the news' as a collection of the most horrific events of the world is not representative of everything that happens in the world in one day. Younger children find it very difficult to understand that the events they are seeing are unlikely to happen to them.

Scary Stuff

It is important for parents and caregivers to remember that television and movies, by their very nature, can expose children to frightening images, events and ideas, many of which they would never experience in their whole lives, without such exposure. Children see and interpret film and TV content differently from adults, and the impact of scary content can have a quite powerful and lasting impact on children. Exposure to scary content can result in short term effects such as intense fear and crying, and longer term effects such as sleep disturbance, refusal to be alone, concern about being hurt or killed, and dependence on unusual bedtime rituals. Long term disabling fears (for example, of dogs, cats and spiders) can emerge.

What is scary in early childhood (under 7 or 8 years)

— scary visual images. For example, vicious animals, monsters, grotesque, mutilated or deformed characters.

— physical transformations of character, particularly when a normal character becomes abnormal or grotesque.

— stories involving the death of a parent

— stories involving natural disasters, shown vividly.

What is scary in the primary years (7-12 years)

— more realistic threats and dangers , especially those which could really happen to a child

— violence, or the threat of violence

— stories in which children are hurt or threatened.

What is scary in early adolescence (13 years and up)

— realistic physical harm or threats of intense harm

— molestation or sexual assault

— threats from aliens or the occult.

Precautions

— Avoid programs with scary stuff. Choose programs or films that are classified as suitable for the age group of your child.

— Keep the TV or VCR out of the child's bedroom

— *What parents can do after the event*

For preschoolers

— take them away from the scary situation

— be sympathetic about the fear

— be with them and provide comfort and attention

— divert them with a drink or a snack

— remember that explanations won't help much.

For older children

— if the program is a fantasy, help them to understand that fantasy things don't happen

— for real threats: tell children that "it's never happened here".

— be sympathetic to their fears

— seek your child's cooperation in avoiding similar exposure

— seek professional help if fears become uncontrollable.

Dealing with Harms

Children may have been exposed to scary or violent material on television, film or video. However, the events of September 11 have brought to many people's attention that children can also be traumatised by being exposed to reports and images from frightening world events. For each age group below there are tips for dealing with both kinds of media trauma.

The reaction of children to scary or violent material will depend to some extent on factors such as:

— individual personality traits such as their sensitivity, vividness of their imagination, susceptibility to visual images, loud noises or 'mood provoking' music
— the media on which the material has been viewed
— whether or not they are with trusted adults at the time.

In general though:

— fear is an intense concern or worry caused by real and/or imagined danger
— children younger than five years old cannot always tell fantasy from reality. Media depictions of attacks can be as scary as real attacks
— all children, even the very young, have a sixth sense that enables them to be aware of an adult's fear and anxiety
— children will respond differently at different ages.

Some children will exhibit fear through behavior, not words. Behaviours that could alert you to the fact that they may have been exposed to scary material are crying, abnormal fussiness or agitation, sleep disturbance, bed wetting, unusually clingy behaviours and greater than normal sensitivity. At the extreme end, there are documented cases of children being so traumatised by viewing violent material that they have had to receive inpatient psychiatric treatment.

If you are with your child at the time that they are exposed to scary or violent material, the more immediate your response the better, in the first instance calmly removing them from the situation. Following this, or if you become aware that your child is reacting to something they saw while you were not with them, the best overall strategy is to acknowledge their fear and reassure them:

— take your cues from the child. Don't assume they are more afraid than they may be. Conversely, don't assume that they are unaware of what has happened.

— take their fears seriously. Don't try to talk them out of it.

— respond calmly. Don't exaggerate their fears by using extreme language or by overreacting.

— answer their questions directly but don't give them more information than they are asking for or that they need

— provide physical reassurance with lots of hugs and touching

— make sure they know that it's okay to ask questions

— manage the media diet of coverage according to their age.

Babies and toddlers

Provide assistance to your child as soon as possible after the event in the following ways:

Scary or violent material on television, film or video

— understand that behaviour problems may be part of their response and give extra reassurance and support

— give lots of physical reassurance.

Violent local or international events as shown on TV News or current affairs programs

In addition to the general tips above, you can help your child at these times in the following ways:

— shield babies and toddlers from media reports as much as possible

— be aware that it is very hard for young children to make sense out of what they see and hear and this can make what they see even more frightening.

— be aware that sensational and disturbing images may be repeated many times and keep the TV and radio off while your children are at home. Repeated viewings will only make the situation worse.

— try not to show your own anxiety because children will quickly pick up your feelings and know there is something wrong. While they won't know exactly what is going on, very young babies and toddlers may pick up a parent's worry and anxiety with their "sixth sense."

Preschoolers

Provide assistance to your child as soon as possible after the event in the following ways:

Scary or violent material on television, film or video

— listen to their feelings and encourage them to talk about them

— give lots of physical reassurance. Understand that the child will need more comfort, especially at bedtime.

— keep to normal routines, which give young children a sense of safety and security.

— give lots of opportunities to play, draw and paint (without guiding them). This helps children to deal with feelings.

— understand that behaviour problems may be part of their response and give extra reassurance and support.

Violent local or international events as shown on TV News or current affairs programs

Preschoolers may be quite tuned in to what has happened. They have probably heard or seen media reports and have probably heard others discussing the events. Preschoolers are most concerned about their own safety and the safety of their parents, relatives and friends. They are not always able to distinguish between fantasy and reality.

In addition to the general tips above, you can help your child at these times in the following ways:

— be aware that it is very hard for young children to make sense out of what they see and hear and this can make what they see even more frightening.

— be aware that sensational and disturbing images may be repeated many times and keep the TV and radio off while your children are at home. Repeated viewings will only make the situation worse.

— try not to discuss what has happened in front of the children

— calmly explain that what has happened is in another country and a long way away and reassure them that they are still safe.

— acknowledge that something very scary has happened, but that you and other adults will make sure they are safe. Let them know that adults will figure out what is going on.

— try not to show your own anxiety because children will quickly pick up your feelings and know there is something wrong.

Early primary school

Provide assistance to your child as soon as possible after the event in the following ways:

Scary or violent material on television, film or video

School age children may still show worries through behaviour as well as or instead of talking about them. They may show them by not wanting to go to school, by behaviour problems or by physical symptoms such as headaches or tummy aches.

A lot of the above suggestions for helping pre-school children will still be appropriate for school age children. In addition:

— give them lots of opportunities to talk about their feelings and their fears. Bedtime is often a good listening time.

— validate their feelings as real.

— let them know they can talk to you any time they are afraid.

Violent local or international events as shown on TV News or current affairs programs

In addition to the general tips above, you can help your child at these times in the following ways:

— a child of this age will be more aware of what is going on and the reactions of other people. They will feel a great deal of concern for their own safety and safety of family and friends.

- — limit TV coverage. Visual images can have a powerful impact. If they ask questions give them information without unnecessary detail.
- — it is important to be honest with them. Tell them what you know about what happened without exaggerating or overreacting. Don't assume that they are too young to know what is going on.
- — acknowledge that something very scary has happened.
- — emphasise that they are safe and that adults will find out what is happening.
- — keep to routines that provide a sense of safety. Some things you can do in the time when you usually watch TV might be playing games, walking the dog, shopping, gardening, a bike ride things that give your family a sense of togetherness.
- — try to help them with their fears by talking through the issues according to their age and understanding eg "Sad and scary things do happen in the world but they are rare and there are lots of sensible people who are working to stop things like this happening".
- — most of all think about your own response. Frightening world events such as September 11 tap into our own sense of insecurity. It is really important to hold on to the sane and down to earth aspects of our daily life and this is what will make the world feel safe for your children.

Upper primary school

A lot of the above suggestions for helping lower primary school children will still be appropriate when they are in upper primary school. In addition:

Scary or violent material on television, film or video

— it is still important to acknowledge and talk through their feelings

— explore their capacity to start applying rational thinking to what they have seen.

Violent local or international events as shown on TV News or current affairs programs

In addition to the general tips above, you can help your child at these times in the following ways:

— children this age will be very aware of what is going on. They may be prone to exaggeration. Jokes or humour can mask fears for this age group.

— talk to your child and answer any questions.

— acknowledge any feelings of fear, horror, and anger.

— provide comfort and reassurance.

— children this age will be more interested in details. Share what you know but don't overwhelm them.

— some children may act out scary feelings or may become more withdrawn. Talk with them and ask them to tell you about their feelings.

— use historical examples (e.g. World Wars, Challenger Space Shuttle, etc.) to explain that bad things happen to innocent people.

High School

Even young people can show their feelings by their behaviour and may withdraw or become aggressive under stress. Provide assistance in the following ways:

Scary or violent material on television, film or video

— it is important to react to the feelings b ınd the behaviour rather than the behaviour itsel

— discuss what they have seen and point out the tricks used to achieve the effects

— respond to their feelings but also appeal to their rational abilities to comprehend.

Violent local or international events as shown on TV News or current affairs programs

In addition to the general tips above, you can help your child at these times in the following ways:

— young people are very aware of what is happening in the world and often very vulnerable

— it is important to talk about what has happened, to listen to their feelings and share yours, but remember they are looking to you and your response for their own sense of safety.

— remember that reactions to a crisis such as this may continue or come back after the media response has died down

— young people in high school have probably already talked about the attacks with friends. It is important to be honest with them and let them know what is going on. This age may be glued to TV, eager for news and details.

— acknowledge fear, sadness, and anger.

— some teens may also just block out the whole thing and refuse to acknowledge that anything big has happened or that they care. This often masks real fears and feelings of being overwhelmed.

— some teens may make jokes. Let them know it's not funny without lecturing them.

— some teens may be very interested in discussing issues that this tragedy raises. Be willing to engage them in serious discussions.

— be careful to avoid placing blame on a whole group of people or targeting particular groups.

— use historical tragedies as a basis for conversation. Talk to your teen about how the situation may be resolved in terms of rescue workers, governmental responses, foreign policy changes, etc.

Managing your own response to world tragedy

— it is important that adults also support each other. Talk about your feelings with friends.

— remember that there are many, many people working together to make the world a better place, and there will be many heroic deeds happening during this crisis that will not be seen on TV but which attest to the sane and good forces in the world

— keep up your usual routines and things you enjoy

— try not to watch too much TV!

— remember that you are the rock for your children no matter what their age. If you keep calm and caring they will usually be OK.

— if necessary seek help—if you are worried about your own or a child's immediate or ongoing reactions seek professional help.

Effects of Violence

Violence in the media is easily accessible to children. It occurs in cartoons, in news updates in family programs, in the news, in "cop shows", and in "blockbuster" movies screened on TV. Many computer games feature violent themes. Trailers for forthcoming programs on TV often contain a collection of the most violent scenes. Parents often feel ambushed by these as they cannot be anticipated.

There have been few content analyses done on TV or media for levels of violence. Overseas content analyses, which have some relevance as much of our programming, particularly on commercial TV is from the US, show that children's cartoons carry the most acts of violence.

Violence in the media is all pervasive, and difficult to avoid. Frequently the violence is glamorised , and violent solutions offer the way to be powerful. Mostly the heroes are male, and the victims are female, showing who does the violence and to whom it's done. Violent media and products are actively marketed to children and young people. The products themselves are frequently in a classification not recommended for children. There is much cross promotion of violent products, e.g. by fast food chains and cinema links; toys and TV series; toys and cinema films.

The Australian Psychological Society has this to say about media violence in a July 2000 Position Paper:

> "For at least 20 years there has been a consensus amongst most of the psychological research community actively involved in media research that violence on television contributes to aggressive behaviour, to anxiety about becoming a victim and to callousness with respect to the impact of violence on others. Studies have predominantly, but not

> exclusively, focused on children. The evidence for these links is as strong as that for the contribution of any other studied contributor to community violence."

Four major US medical groups (the American Academy of Pediatrics, American Psychological Association, American Academy of Child and Adolescent Psychiatry and American Medical) issued a joint statement in 2000 entitled Joint Statement on the Impact of Entertainment Violence on Children: Congressional Public Health Summit. They summarised their position as follows:

— Children who see a lot of violence are more likely to view violence as an effective way of settling conflicts. Children exposed to violence are more likely to assume that acts of violence are acceptable behaviour

— Viewing violence can lead to emotional desensitization towards violence in real life. It can decrease the likelihood that one will take action on behalf of a victim when violence occurs.

— Entertainment violence feeds a perception that the world is a violent and mean place. Viewing violence increases fear of becoming a victim of violence, with a resultant increase in self-protective behaviours and a mistrust of others.

— Viewing violence may lead to real life violence. Children exposed to violent programming at a young age have a higher tendency for violent and aggressive behaviour later in life than children whoa are not so exposed.

We can learn much about the way in which media violence will impact on the young from the solid base of child development research and theory developed over 50 years. Findings from social science research on specific topics can be used to supplement this knowledge. Some researchers dispute that media violence has a detrimental impact on the young, but there are now over 200 original research studies and many more research reviews which combine to give a reliable picture of the likely impact of violent media on children.

US researcher Craig Anderson (who has conducted both original research on media violence (especially computer games) and carried out meta-analyses of the mass of research studies) sums up the situation in regard to the research evidence in this way:

> "The effect of media violence on aggression in general is bigger than the effect of smoking on lung cancer; it's bigger than the effect of calcium intake on bone mass; it's bigger than the effect of homework on academic achievement, or the effect of asbestos exposure on lung cancer. These are all effects that people generally understand to be true, real effects that are large enough to be important and large enough to worry about".

In summary, the research shows us that a diet of media violence can increase the risks that children will:

— be more likely to choose to use violence to solve conflict

— be desensitised to use of violence by others (more callous)

— develop a mean and scary view of the world.

The risks are increased when children's real life experiences are close to those on the media. Further, the impact of violent media is likely to be increased when the child viewer spends time fantasising about the program afterwards. (i.e. by playing with toys linked to the violent program). The research also gives us good indicators as to the types of media violence that will increase the three risks outlined above.

The risk of choosing violence to solve conflict is increased by exposure to programs in which the violence is performed by an attractive hero, who does violence in a good cause, who is rewarded and applauded for doing it, whose violence has few real life consequences, and is set in a comic context.

The risk of being desensitised to the use of violence by others is increased by exposure to movies in which graphic violence is shown constantly and humorously.

The risk of developing a mean and scary view of the world is increased when children see programs, such as the news, in which violence happens to real people, to children and animals, and they fear that such things will happen to them.

The research tells us that the most vulnerable to media violence are:

— children under the age of seven or eight. Children of this age find it difficult to distinguish between fantasy and reality. To the young child, even a cartoon hero can be seen as real, especially when the characters resemble real people (as opposed to Daffy Duck or Bugs Bunny). Young children tend to watch a lot of cartoon series in which the major theme is that of resolution or winning by using violence.

— boys (because most violence in the media is done by males)

— those who live in violent homes

— those who spend a lot of time with media.

Older children (over eight) are more likely to be upset by the news because they know it is about real life and can identify with some of the settings and happenings.

Boys seem to be more vulnerable to violent media portrayals than girls. This is seen to because there are many male role models in the media, and most of these succeed by best at doing the violence. Boys are interested in seeing how to be powerful.

Frequent exposure to violent products will increase the risks that children will develop a mental script for the way to deal with conflict, and this may not emerge until later in life. Children's media environment contains much of the harmful forms of glamorised violence. This poses a serious mental health risk for society. Media violence is but one contributor to the use of violence in society, but it is one that we can do something about.

Precautions

Parents can:

— Minimise exposure to programs and products which feature glamourised violence.

— Minimise exposure to news programs for children under 11 or 12. These children are unlikely to understand that "it isn't likely to happen to you" as they don't understand probability

— *Be a media educator*: express your views, and discuss program content for example talk to children about what would happen if they did those violent things at home

— Buy or borrow videos with themes other than violence.

Short term and long term effects

The impact of violence in the media on a child will depend on a number of factors:

- the age of the child
- the sex of the child
- the individual sensitivities of the child
- whether the child is well supported by a parent who talks to the child about what he sees
- whether the child lives in a home where violent behaviour is condoned
- whether the child spends time fantasising about what he's seen (including playing with toys related to a violent program)
- the amount of time that the child spends with programs with themes of violence
- the types of violence seen in the program. For example, whether the violence is "glamorised" (attractive violent heroes who are rewarded for violence, and the violence has few real life consequences).

Impact on Children under 8

- are likely to imitate the violence seen in programs in their play. They don't easily understand the difference between fantasy and reality, and may not realise that imitation is dangerous. Children have been known to be able to reproduce violent acts seen on TV some months earlier.
- are likely to be very scared by "scary" images, for example scary faces, sinister music and sounds, and

"transformations" (remember the Incredible Hulk?). Young children will not be able to tell themselves that the scary thing will go away soon (as older children can). The impact of scary images may result in fear of being alone, may result in nightmares, or in long term fears.

— may develop a "script" for ways of solving conflict that may not emerge until later in life.

Impact on School aged children (8-12)

— are likely to be disturbed by short term exposure to violence in the news, especially when the violence looks like it could have happened in his neighbourhood. This is because older children are likely to relate to and identify with familiar settings and fear that those things could happen to them. For example, a young girl may fear being kidnapped because she has seen a report where a young girl suffered that fate. Explaining that it isn't likely to happen , is not of much use to a child who is not of an age to understand probability.

— will be influenced by long term exposure to films and movies which feature real heroes. If these heroes consistently use violence to win, if it's rewarded, if it has few real life consequences and is also in a humorous context, this is likely to increase the risk. With long term exposure, children are more likely to choose to use violence to solve conflict than if not so exposed.

— may become desensitised to (or more callous about) the use of violence by others. This effect tends to result from long term exposure to violence which is realistic, (much blood and gore) and which is in a humorous context.

Precautions to be taken by the Parents

The under 8 year old

— avoid exposure to violent cartoons and reality based programs

— avoid programs with easily copied violent actions

— avoid buying violent toys related to TV programs

— select programs that are appropriate for their age

— keep a store of taped programs that are age appropriate

— limit time with TV and other media

— provide comfort and support when the child has been frightened.

The primary school aged child

— help them select programs and games that are classified below "M 15+"

— help them select programs and games which do not feature (or provide the opportunity to be) the hero who does "glamorised" violence

— encourage supporting and caring behaviour, and discourage aggressive behaviour

— help them to be critical viewers, and talk to them about your reasons for avoiding certain programs

— discuss and explain the meaning of televised events

— modify your own viewing.

While there may be many entertaining experiences for children to be had on TV, with videos, and with computers, it is important to keep in mind what children of different ages need for healthy development. It is important that children have time to be in the real world, and to build strong bonds with real caring people. Media can be a thief of children's time that they really need for other experiences—active physical play and "hands-on" activities of all kinds. Children need experiences that enhance their development, and all too frequently media content fails to do that. Keeping children's media time down can reduce the impact of programs and games where harmful messages are constantly repeated.

— *Children under the age of two years:* The most important developmental task that children have in this age group is to develop strong relationships with their carers. They need to be close, feel loved and talked to. The American Academy of Pediatrics has recommended that screen based media should occupy very little of the time of infants.

— *Preschoolers:* These children are starting to explore the world more actively. They need constructive play activities, and need to feel secure, loved and valued. When they watch TV, they focus on the most physically obvious features of TV programs, and rarely follow plots. They need programs that are specifically made for pre school children. An hour of TV a day is plenty.

— *Children from the age of five to seven or eight years of age:* These children don't easily distinguish between fantasy and reality, and are vulnerable to the messages conveyed in cartoons, and advertisements. An hour a day with screen based media is plenty.

Impacts of Advertising

Advertising directed to children includes paid advertisements or commercials that appear in TV programs specifically made for children or in other programs for children and where the product is principally of interest to children under the age of 13 years.

Advertising directed to children occurs:

— in TV programs that are specifically made for children

— in other children's programs (such as cartoon programs), and

— in other programs.

The amount of advertising can be as high as 15 minutes per hour. Sometimes, the descriptions of prizes for a competition, or the demonstration of a product in a cartoon program can be construed as advertising. Such practices should occur in discrete segments within the program. Pay TV also carries advertising directed to children, but at a lower level of minutes per hour. Advertising directed to children also occurs on the Internet e.g. in banner ads.

Many of the products advertised are fatty, salty, sugary and fast foods. Nutritionists and other health professionals see these as promoting poor eating practices in children.

Young children are particularly vulnerable to advertising as they are unable to distinguish advertising from programs. US researchers such as Dale Kunkel and Don Roberts say that children under age of 5 or 6 do not distinguish effectively between advertisements and the programs they are watching.

Most children six to seven hears of age understand the selling function of advertisements, while most eight year olds understand their specifically persuasive intent. They expressed concern that children are less likely to adopt a critical approach to their processing of advertising intent. Many of the advertisements use techniques that mislead children as to the worth or performance of the product. To understand selling intent, the child has to be able to take the perspective of another, and to understand that the seller will engage in puffery, trickery, exaggeration in order to sell.

Children are effective influencers of family purchasers, pestering their parents to buy products that they neither need nor really understand. A British study reported that 85% of a sample of 4-13 year olds acknowledged that they had asked their parents to buy advertised products and 66% claimed that their parents had met their request.

Advertising pressures can produce significant conflict between parents and children. Many vulnerable families succumb, spending dollars they can least afford. Pester power often works.

Advertising to children is an unfair practice. HIt works by making you unhappy with their lives, anxious and unsatisfied. It sells to them by damaging their mental health.

Children under the age of 7 or 8 are most vulnerable. Advertising directed as this age group is inherently unfair. But even older children do not always know when advertisements are telling the truth, and are vulnerable to the appeals (as even adults are) to the appeals to their self esteem, anxieties, and need to be seen as "cool".

Big business now runs annual conferences (with big fees) to share the best techniques to sell their products to children. Children are being actively targeted by the advertising industry for three reasons:

— they have considerable money of their own

— they are powerful influencers of family purchases, from breakfast cereal to the family car

— if captured early, can develop a warm and fuzzy feeling towards a company for life.

Food Advertising

Advertisements for food on television occur principally as 30 second commercials within programs directed to children, or within other programs directed at a more general audience. They can also occur by way of "product placement" within programs. Food or drink products are used by the characters in the film, video or TV program, or placed somewhere conspicuous on the set.

Advertisements for foods directed to children are most frequently for breakfast cereals, snacks, soft drinks, and fast foods. They can be described as fatty, salty, sugary and fast. Advertisements at times that children are watching, can occur at the rate of: 30 per hour, or 75 per day, or around 22,000 per year. Food ads, as a percentage of total ads on television, range from 25%-48%, and average 34%. A 13 industrialised-nation study of advertising during children's television viewing times found that Australia recorded the highest number of food ads per hour.

Children are very powerful influencers of family purchases of every thing from the breakfast cereals to the evening meal choices. Many products advertised on television are displayed in the supermarket at child's eye level. Pester power works.

Sophisticated and aggressive techniques are used in marketing to children. Techniques used by television food advertisers include prizes, giveaways, animation, special effects, story vignettes, jingles, and popular personalities. The predominant messages directed to children are related to having fun, being cool and the food being tasty. Young children (under the age of eight years) are very susceptible to advertisements. If an advertisement for a product attracts their interest, they will ask for it even if it is a product for which they have no need or use.

The messages for food ads on TV are encouraging children to the view that what's good to eat is "good for them". In fact, television food ads during children's viewing times disproportionately promote foods of low nutritional value-foods high in fat, sugar or salt. The proportion of ads promoting non-nutritious foods range from 50-84%, and average 72%. The largest categories of foods advertised tend to be chocolate and confectionery, fast food restaurants and sweetened breakfast cereals.

Precautions to be taken by the Parents

Several surveys conducted with the Australian community (including parents) have shown that they are concerned about television food advertising to children; there was consistently strong community opinion in favour of tighter controls of TV food advertising to children.

Parents can:

— limit the amount of commercial TV that their children are exposed to.

— introduce children to a range of tasty foods that are good for them, and which can be fun to eat

— limit the consumption of foods advertised on TV to once or twice a week

— play "spot the gimmicks" in advertisements on TV: encourage your child to be sceptical about claims made in advertisements.

Toy Advertising

Toys are promoted very heavily to children through a wide range of media. They are presented in such a way as to make them look very attractive and great fun to play with. The children shown playing with them are cute, pretty or "cool".

Many such toys are very expensive. Toys advertised on TV or otherwise linked to movies tend to dominate children's "wish lists" for presents. Early childhood educators have expressed concern that many of the media-promoted toys do not extend children's play, but limit it. Children can get much enjoyment from other simpler and cheaper toys. These days, many mass produced toys are not designed to meet the needs of children, but more to meet the objectives of a range of industries who are jointly marketing to children.

Toys are promoted on television, by promotional segments within television programs, spin-offs from movies, and links with fast food chains. Other methods include "virus marketing".

— *On television:* Children are exposed to toy advertising on television. Children watching commercial children's television see up to 15 minutes per hour of commercials (that is, about 30 commercials per hour) for a range of products including toys (and especially in the pre Christmas season).

Toys are promoted to children via television in a variety of other ways as well. These include links with fast food chains (as premium offers), via toy-linked cartoon series, spin-off products from children' programs, and via hosted segments within television programs.

— *Cinema films:* Children are exposed to spin-offs from cinema films.

— *Virus marketing*: This method involves the selection of the most "cool" kid in the school or club, and supplying him or her with a free new toy or gadget. The child's prestige as a leader provides the stimulus for other children to want the toy or gadget as well.

Toys and trinkets are very frequently advertised as part of a commercial for another product (for eg fast food outlets). An example would be the fast food meal offer which includes a toy for the child. The trinket or toy is called a "premium offer". Parents often get pressured to go to a fast food chain in order for the child to get the offer.

In many cases, children's television cartoon series are devised principally as vehicles for "bringing to life" a toy or range of toys. The toys existed first and the cartoon series was produced afterwards. Examples include Teenage Mutant Ninja Turtles, Transformers, Mighty Morphin Power Rangers, Action Man, Pokemon. The list is endless.

The move to produce toy linked cartoon series began in the US in 1984 when the USA Federal Trade Commission deregulated children's television and discontinued a prohibition against toy linked cartoon series. He Man and the Masters of the Universe was the first such series produced and began an avalanche of such series all over the world. These series are cheap for television stations to obtain, being either subsidised, or screened with the promise of associated toy advertising.

There are some rules that limit the ability of hosts or characters in children's television programs from promoting products within the program. Fore exampe, the Commercial TV Australia Code of Practice para 6.23 requires that in any program mainly directed to children:

— the host or other regular presenter or character in the program must not sell or promote products or services

— products that have names or packaging featuring the host or 'any other regular presenter or character within the program must not be recommended or promoted within the program

— material within the program which recommends or promotes products or services, must be presented as discrete segments, and its sponsorship must be clear

— references to prizes for competitions must be brief.

Toys are commonly part of the spin-off merchandise from many children's shows, and cinema films these days. Most such spin-offs are planned as an integral part of the cross media promotion for the movie or program. In some rare instances, the money generated by the spin-off goes back to keeping the program on air.

There are no rules that prohibit or limit toy-linked cartoons series, or the spin-offs from movies. Some problems for children from toy linked television series and movies:

— these series increase the difficulties that young children under the age of five already have in distinguishing between programs and commercials. In toy linked television series, the program and "advertising" content are intertwined.

— the child is encouraged to want the toys associated with the characters in the series. It's usually a whole team of toys rather than just one, and play is not seen as satisfactory unless the child has the whole team.

— the toys are frequently related to violent cartoon series (due to the ease of making spectacular action and effects), and via the plots, the child is encouraged to play with them violently.

— findings from research indicates that the amount of time that a child spends fantasising about violent acts he or she has seen by playing with the toys, wearing the T shirt etc, is likely to increase the impact of the violence.

— the "hyper-commercialisation" of children's toys, through the collaboration of several industries to use children to promote their products, often results in toys which do not meet children's real play needs.

— the pressure to create series that meet toy manufacturers needs rather than children's, often results in stereotyped story lines, and the consequent limiting of children' story worlds.

Precautions to be taken by the Parents

— minimise young children's exposure to commercial media

— build a selection of non-toy related videos

— be an active media educator. Show children the real toy when you're out shopping and point out differences between the television ad and the real thing. Talk about the tricks used in advertising.

— choose age specific toys that meet children's real play needs.

Effects of Advertising on children's health

TV watching is a major activity for children and adolescents. If a child watches the average of two and a half hours per day and if this is mainly commercial TV he or she will see around 75 advertisements in a day, or around 22,000 per year. Advertising often works by making us feel unhappy with our lives, anxious and dissatisfied. The messages are that you are not OK unless you buy this, wear that brand, wash your hair with, and look like that very slim model. It attacks our self esteem.

What are the particular problems for children and young people:

— girls in early adolescence are particularly vulnerable to messages about being OK as they are sensitive about their body image and whether they measure up to the peer group

— recent research indicates that there is a marked link between TV watching, and negative body and eating disorders.

— television advertising featuring idealised thinness negatively affected both the mood and the body image of adolescent girls, with those in the 13 - 15 year age group being more affected.

Precautions to be taken by the Parents

— from an early age give your children a solid sense of their worth and encourage them to have high self esteem, by valuing them for what they are, and as they are

— minimise children's exposure to commercial TV in the early years. Anxieties created by advertising start early

— act as media educators from an early age, pointing out the techniques used in advertising, and discussing how people in the TV world look compared to how most of us do

— encourage media education at your children's schools, so that children are well equipped to read the media.

Increasingly, there are very sophisticated marketing campaigns directed to children, and at a younger and younger age. While it is almost impossible for parents to keep their children away from advertising and marketing pressures, there are a number of constructive things that parents can do to modify the impact of these. We all need to remember that advertising works by making us feel unhappy with our lives-anxious and unsatisfied. Successful campaigns will work by making us feel that life will be better, and we will be happier if we buy, wear, wash our hair with, eat certain things. Advertising to children will play on their insecurities and need for acceptance by their peers.

The best defence against advertising that we can give our children right from birth, is a solid sense of self-esteem. Then there are some other more immediate steps that we can take:

— minimise young children's (under the age of eight years) exposure to commercial media

— build a selection of videos that don't promote a line of toys along the way

— be an active media educator. Show children the real toy when you're out shopping and point out differences between the TV ad and the real thing. With older children, talk about the tricks used in advertising, and show them how much more the heavily sugared and promoted cereals cost in comparison to the less advertised ones.

— don't give TV or movie related toys as presents; don't buy foods advertised on TV

— choose age specific toys that meet children's real play needs.

Physical Effects of Media Use

The impact of using screen media (TV, videos, computers and computer games) on children's physical health has a number of aspects. These aspects include direct impacts of prolonged use such as:

— eyestrain

— repetitive strain injury

— postural problems

There may also for some children be risks relating to:

— epilepsy

— electro magnetic radiation (EMR)

There are also displacement effects, that is, that computer use can displace involvement in physical activity.

Eyestrain: Gazing for long periods at a screen should be avoided. Focus should be shifted frequently to other objects in the room. Occupational health and safety guidelines indicate a break of ten minutes should be taken every hour, away from the screen. .When watching TV, the conventional wisdom is that a child should not sit closer than two meters from the screen.

Repetitive strain injury: This can arise from overuse of a keyboard or spending too much time pressing buttons on a video game. Keyboards should be adjusted so that the forearms are not raised at an angle.

Postural problems: Care should be taken to ensure that seating supports the back; the neck is not arched back; the keyboard is adjusted so that the arms are not raised at an angle; and the feet are supported (ie on an angled stool). If posture is poor while using computers for long periods, neck, back and posture problems can occur.

Electro magnetic radiation (EMR): Closeness to any electrical appliance that is switched on exposes one to electro-magnetic radiation. Argument rages on what levels are safe and what are not, but a cautious approach suggests that less is better, particularly for children who tend to be more vulnerable to almost any form of pollution.

Epilepsy: Makers of video games warn that playing the games can cause attacks of epilepsy in susceptible individuals. This warning is supported by recent research.

Lack of physical activity: If children spend long hours in front of the TV and /or the computer, they are likely to have less time for physical activity.

In addition, daily hours of commercial TV will include a high level of advertisements for fatty, salty, sugary and fast foods. These can influence children's attitudes in the direction of "what's good to eat" rather than "what's good for them". Children also tend to snack while watching TV. The impact of hours at the TV set and eating frequently advertised foods is contributing to a rising problem of obesity in children.

Role Computers and Video Games in Child Growth

Computer and video games were first developed in the 1970s. As technology and programming improved, games became more accessible to individuals in their own homes and the industry experienced massive growth. Computer and video games are programs that are designed for recreational use. They can be used on a variety of platforms, that is on many different types of machines, systems or devices. Games can be bought or downloaded from the internet. You can play games on:

— a computer, either Mac or PC

— home consoles used with TV sets.

— oin-operated arcade game machines

— handheld game systems.

Various types of games are:

— *first person shooter (3D Action, shooter, FPS)*. The player holds the gun and shoots other characters. Always violent. Examples are Quake, Unreal, Soldier of Fortune, Medal of Honour, Return to Castle Wolfenstein, Grand Theft Auto: Vice City, Vietcong, Battlefield 1942.

— *COMBAT*. The player's character competes physically, often through martial arts, with other characters. Always violent. Examples are Mortal Kombat, Tekken.

— *real-time strategy (RTS).* The player can strategically direct battles. Always violent, but not usually graphic. Examples are: Age of Empires, Command & Conquer, Close Combat.

— *role playing.* The player goes on a quest of some sort overcoming obstacles on the way. Usually violent.

— *adventure.* The player follows clues or uses problem-solving to overcome obstacles and puzzles which must be solved to continue the story. Can be set in fantasy worlds or ancient times. Rarely violent. Examples are: Myst, Syberia, Dark Fall, Monkey Island.

— *simulators* — sports, racing or aircraft flight. The player participates in simulated sporting situations, car races or flies an aircraft. Some are violent. Examples are: Links, Sports Car G2, V8 Super Cars, Flight Simulator.

— *platform.* Relatively simple games, often made for young children. The player chases or avoids characters by jumping onto platforms. Examples are Super Mario Brothers, Sonic the Hedgehog, Donkey Kong.

There are many benefits available to children and adults who use computer and video games in a healthy way. In addition to providing entertainment, some games can:

— introduce children to computer technology

— give practice in following directions, problem solving and logic, use of fine motor and spatial skills, visual skills

— provide occasions for parents and children to play together.

There are many risks associated with computer and video games, which include:

— becoming addicted

— being exposed to violence, particularly practising violent acts in the first person

— developing or reinforcing negative racial or sexual stereotypes.

Becoming addicted: Often children can become 'hooked' into the fast moving world of computer games. Excessive exposure to games can lead to a number of problems, such as poor eating habits, not mixing with others, poor communication, trouble with school work, social isolation and not paying attention in class.

A child who is cutting back on:

— the time they spend outside

— being with friends

— playing sports

— other social or club activities

— in order to spend more time playing computer and video games may be at risk of developing an addiction.

Exposure to violence: There is a growing body of research which indicates that playing computer games where violence is the major theme, is harmful to children. Studies find a relationship between violent television watching and behaviour. Practising violent acts by playing computer games may contribute more to aggressive behaviour than passive television watching.

Game environments are often based on plots of violence, aggression and gender bias. Playing violent video games may be related to aggressive behaviour. In many violent games, players must become more violent to win. In first person shooter games, the player may be more affected because he or she controls the game and experiences the action through the eyes of his or her character. Some claim playing violent video games provides an outlet for aggression. This view is not supported by the research.

Development or reinforcement of negative stereotypes: Women are often portrayed as weaker characters that are helpless or sexually provocative. Villains are often portrayed as coming from ethnic backgrounds other than Anglo Saxon.

It is helpful to be clear in your own mind about the potential impact of computer and video games. Dr Craig Anderson, one of the leading researchers on video game violence, has produced a simple three point summary, stating:

— learning happens

— content matters

— venting (the theory that players get rid of angry feelings when they play computer games) doesn't work.

It is important to be aware of what games your children are playing. Get involved in purchases they are making and use the classification to guide their choices. Learn as much as possible about the games, perhaps even playing them with your children. Make clear rules about what games are and are not acceptable in your home and the amount of time children are allowed to play them.

Computer games can provide endless hours of fun for children, and can offer many interesting and challenging experiences. The problem is that far too many games have central themes of violence. In violent computer and computer games, the child player needs to perform acts of violence to achieve the end goal of the game (for example to use an electronic gun to kill opponents). The child is actively encouraged to identify with the aggressive hero and to rehearse aggressive acts, and is rewarded for doing so. The person who is best at the violence wins.

What is the likely impact on children of playing such games

— teachers and child developmentalists tell us that children learn better by doing than watching; it could be argued that a child playing a violent computer and video game will learn the success of being violent from those games.

— being rewarded for performing violence is likely to increase the impact.

— violent computer and video games teach skills in "point and shoot" techniques. The games can help in overcoming the natural reluctance that most people feel in pointing at and shooting another human being.

— research is now starting to show that playing violent games increases the child's willingness to use violence to solve conflict. Recent reviews of the research literature reveal that violent video games increases aggressive behaviour in children and young adults.

Precautions to be taken by the Parents

— help children avoid computer games which have a focus on violence

— choose games that have positive themes

— help children understand and use the classification system, and choose games that are classified G or G8.

— place the computer in a public area of the house and not in the child's bedroom; join in sometimes

— place limits on the amount of time with screen based media. Children need time for other activities in the real world.

Dr Craig Anderson, one of the leading researchers on video game violence, has compiled a checklist for parents to help them avoid purchasing video games that have features, which research suggests, can cause harm. He suggests the following ways to tell if a game is potentially harmful:

1. Play the game yourself, or have someone demonstrate it for you

2. Ask yourself the following questions:

   Does the game involve some characters trying to harm others?

   Does this happen frequently, that is, more than once or twice in 30 minutes?

   Is the harm rewarded in any way?

   Is the harm depicted as humorous?

   Are non-violent solutions absent or less fun than the violent ones?

Are realistic consequences of violence absent from the game?

If the answers to two or more questions is "yes", think very carefully about the lessons being taught before allowing access to those games.

Computer and video games are programs that are designed for recreational use. They can be used on a variety of platforms, that is on many different types of machines, systems or devices. Many children get a lot of enjoyment out of playing video games and they can provide a healthy avenue for relieving tension and practising visual, problem-solving and fine motor skills. However, there are dangers associated with computer and video game use.

It is helpful to be clear in your own mind about the potential impact of computer and video games. Dr Craig Anderson, one of the leading researchers on video game violence, has produced a simple three point summary, stating:

— learning happens

— content matters

— venting (the theory that players get rid of angry feelings when they play computer games) doesn't work.

Research indicates that:

— children are more likely to learn that violence is an acceptable way to solve conflict if the violent behaviour is rewarded.

— children need to learn that violent behaviour does have consequences.

— the more graphic the violence, the greater the impact.

— practising violence against other humans teaches at some level that violence against others is OK.

— sexual violence can be dangerous learning, particularly for adolescent boys who are at the developmental stage of learning how to relate to women.

Be aware that computer and video games are big business and that they are being actively marketed to your children. What might seem harmless entertainment can actually be very harmful to preschoolers, yet even adults can sometimes be 'tricked' into thinking some games and programs are suitable for families by a combination of clever promotion and advertising.

The following pointers should help you in choosing good computer and video games.

— *Check the cover of the game*: If the title and picture on the cover of the game include violence and sexual themes, you can assume these themes are also in the game. All video covers (for sale or hire) must clearly display the Office of Film and Literature Classification (OFLC) rating and consumer advice lines.

— *Use the OFLC classification system*: In Australia, by law, all computer and video games (including those in arcades) have to be classified by the Office of Film and Literature Classification (OFLC). Video covers and arcade booths must clearly display the game's classification and 'consumer advice' which indicates the chief reasons why the game got its classification (for example 'medium level violence').

— *Rent and preview the game before purchasing:* Before allowing your child to purchase a computer game, rent the game and preview it with your child.

— *Look for games which provide constructive learning*: Once you have eliminated games that have violent or sexual themes, look for games that provide constructive learning experiences, games that:

  — are more complex that punching, running, jumping or shooting

  — encourage group activity

  — require the player to come up with strategies, solve problems and make decisions.

Even though you have taken care in choosing appropriate computer and video games for your child, there are a number of ways that you can continue to exert a positive influence.

Make sensible rules about playing computer games: Parents can make a big difference in reducing the risks for their children by making sensible rules. Be clear with them about what is acceptable content and what you will not allow them to play. It is helpful for the child if they have the opportunity to discuss with you your reasons. Depending on the age of the child, you may choose to negotiate with them:

— how much time can be spent playing computer games, setting a daily or weekly limit

— times at which they are not allowed to play, for example during meal times or after a certain time at night

— what other activities need to be completed before playing computer games, for example, homework, sport or music practice, household chores.

Keep the computer in a public place: In this way you can more easily monitor how much time your child is spending playing games and the content of the games they are playing.

Monitor what your children are playing: As much as possible, keep track of the games your children are playing. Find out where they get games from: in addition to buying or hiring them they could be getting them from friends, off the internet or from contacts they have made on the internet. Exposure to violent and sexually explicit computer games and images has been linked to emotional and health problems in children. As with purchasing games, it is a good idea tc check games that your child has got from other sources yourself, particularly if the game has themes of violence and / or sex.

Discuss what they are playing elsewhere: It is likely that your child will be exposed to many games that you would not allow in your own home, either at friends' homes or in arcades. Use the opportunity to explain to your child the potentially harmful effect of playing such games.

Keep communication open: Listen to what your child has to say about the computer and video games they are playing. Explain the reasons for your viewpoint, encourage them to question the marketing surrounding the computer game industry and to start making informed decisions for themselves.

Keep an eye on your child's overall health and wellbeing: Take note of your child's reactions after they have been playing computer games.

Watch out for signs that your child is becoming addicted to playing computer games. Changes in eating habits, moods, school performance, interaction with friends and involvement in non-computer activities might indicate that a problem is developing.

5

Children and the Internet

Most children at some stage will use the internet. Many parents, on the other hand, have had little or no exposure. As a result, parents often find it difficult to understand the issues involved and therefore have problems discussing them with their children. The internet is a massive network of computers from around the world all connected by cable and satellite. When users are connected to the internet, they can receive text, images, video and sound on their computer from computers anywhere in the world. Just as there is a book or magazine on nearly every subject in local libraries, bookshops or newsagents, so is there information on virtually every subject on the internet. The internet is sometimes called the world wide web or just 'the net'.

Being on the internet is called being on-line. Playing on the internet or hunting for information is called 'surfing' the net. In 2003 there were about 619 million internet users worldwide and 10.9 million in Australia. You can use 'public access' machines to access the internet free of charge in most public libraries and for a small fee at internet cafes that can be found in most major cities. If you want to have internet access in your own home or workplace you will need:

— a computer

— *a modem*. This is a piece of hardware that enables your computer to connect to your Internet Service Provider (ISP) and from there to other computers.

— *a telephone line*. For home use, many people use their existing telephone line. If you prefer, you can get a separate telephone line connected. (You may also hear terms such as broadband, ADSL, cable, ISDN and satellite in respect to internet connections, but these technologies are at this stage not commonly used for individual computer access.)

— *an Internet Service Provider (ISP)*. ISPs are companies which act as a link between your computer and other computers. To provide this service they have sophisticated hardware and communications software. They charge users a fee for this service and usually provide some level of support.

— *browser software*. Browser software needs to be installed on your computer to enable you to use the world wide web. Currently the most commonly used browser software packages are Netscape Navigator and Internet Explorer. Most newer computers come with browser software automatically installed.

— *email software*. This enables users to send messages to other users. This may come in a package with your browser software or you can buy it separately. Some commonly used emailing software packages are Netscape Messenger, Eudora, Outlook and Outlook Express.

When you connect to the internet, you are effectively making a phone call. Using your modem, your computer dials out and connects through your ISP to the internet. If your ISP is in the same State as you, the cost of connection is the same as the cost of a local phone call. Your ISP charges are in addition to the phone call charge. Some ISPs have toll-free numbers for users in country and rural areas. Once connected to the internet, there are several features of the internet you can access. You can:

— access information from the world wide web

— send and receive emails

— visit chat rooms

— use instant messaging

— join newsgroups

— view videos and / or listen to radio stations.

Access information from the world wide web: Any individual or organisation can create a 'website' on which they can provide any information they choose to. Information on a website is usually separated in a logical way into 'web pages'. Web pages include: information about a company and its services, promotional materials, information on any topic, reports, facts and figures, links to other relevant websites and so on. The possibilities are endless.

There are two main ways of accessing information on the world wide web. You can:

— go directly to an individual or organisation's 'website'

— use a search engine to locate some information you are looking for, possibly over a number of websites. To use a search engine you don't need to know any specific addresses.

Web address: Each website has a unique address or url. If you know a website address, you can type it in and go directly to that individual's or company's website and access their information. If you visit a particular website frequently, you can set up a 'bookmark' for it, so that you can easily find it again. Depending on your browser, sites you have bookmarked are listed as Bookmarks or Favorites.

Using a search engine: Search engines are tools that are available once you connect to the internet. You enter keywords (search items) relevant to the information you are looking for and the search engine produces a list of websites that contain those keywords. From the list you can select one or more website that you think will be helpful for you. Generally, the more search items you provide, the better your results will be. Some commonly used search engines are Google and Alta Vista.

Once you have found the information you want you can either look at it on screen or 'download' it. Downloading is the term used for saving information from the internet onto your own computer so that you can access it after you have disconnected from the internet. You can download documents, images, software and many other forms of information. You can also print information from the internet.

Once you have gone to a particular website, you will often find links to other websites. In this way you can jump between many websites to look for the information you want. Searching for information by going from one website to another is known as 'surfing'.

Send and receive emails: Email is an electronic form of sending a letter to another person. You can attach documents and photos which arrive at their destination in the same format as you sent them. Email is a very quick and cheap means of communicating and is very widely used. Your ISP will set up an email address for you when you join up with them. If you do not have an ISP, for example if you primarily use public access machines, you can still access emails by setting up a free 'hotmail' account.

Visit chat rooms: Chat rooms (sometimes called chat lines) are a means by which one person can talk (by typing text) to another person or to a group of people. It's like being in a building with hundreds of rooms—you can choose a room by a topic or location and have an open discussion with the people in that room. The people you chat to are from all around the world. From a child's point of view they should be classed as strangers. Some chat rooms are monitored, which makes sure decent language and conduct are maintained. Others are not. Chat lines are very popular with children and young adults.

Join newsgroups: Newsgroups are an electronic bulletin board, accessed by using the same or similar software to your email software. People join news groups of common interest and share ideas and resources on the chosen topic. Some newsgroups are monitored and stick tightly to the topic, whilst others are not and contain adult conversation. Some newsgroups may be used by paedophiles.

View videos and/or listen to radio stations: Viewing videos on-line, listening to radio stations or playing music is making use of 'streaming content'. Streaming content means that you can view activities in other places as they happen, for example, you can see what is happening in Times Square in New York and on the NASA site you can view space shuttle activity. Or you can listen to radio programs as they are broadcast or watch music videos.

Some commonly used streaming content programs are RealMedia, Quicktime and Microsoft Media Player.

On-line video chat is like a chat line but with pictures and voice. A small personal video camera is attached to the computer. These cameras make it possible to see the person you are talking to. Learning more about the internet is a good first step to being able to discuss it with your children. Spending time with your children as they use the internet will help you to learn more and your children may even appreciate the opportunity to be able to teach you something.

Benefits of Internet

The internet can provide children and adults alike with a world of exciting opportunities. It offers:

— educational games and programs

— research information for school projects and business

— the opportunity to communicate with people from all around the world

— the opportunity to share resources and ideas with people that have the same interests

— shopping around the world without leaving your computer.

The internet uses multimedia and interactivity extensively. Using multimedia means that you can access not only written words, but also pictures, music and sound effects. Interactivity means that the user can choose what they want to see just by the click of a mouse. The computer 'asks' users questions which they can then answer.

On-line Dangers

There are no regulations or controls on the material that is placed on the internet. While there are over 3 million perfectly safe children's sites on the net, children can unexpectedly come across material of a sexual or violent nature, language that is rude and the advertising of children's products. Quite innocently they can bring up sites that do not relate to the topic they are looking for, or someone can send them images or messages that are not appropriate. Therefore there are many things on-line that are not suitable for children or that are cause for concern. The main dangers to children are that they may:

— access inappropriate information

— inadvertently form 'friendships' with strangers

— be subjected to advertising pressures

— risk their personal health through excessive use

— endanger their privacy by revealing person details about themselves, such as their name and address.

Access inappropriate information: The search engines on the internet provide access to many sites on a given topic. Even when children are searching for ordinary everyday topics, it is possible that they might come across sites with information and/or images that could be harmful to them.

Sexually explicit material:

— this could include graphic pictures and videos intended for adults

— exposure to graphic pornography can cause emotional distress to children

Violent and disturbing images:

— this could include such things as crash scenes and even mortuary sites

— research has shown that violence in any form of screen media, that is, films, videos, television, computer games and the internet, can have a negative effect on children, particularly young children

Making purchases or gambling online: children can easily come across sites which encourage them to purchase goods on-line on-line gambling. A credit card number is all it takes for someone to 'play'. using 1900 numbers. Children can inadvertently accumulate very large telephone bills in a short space of time by accessing Internet Dialer numbers that transfer them to an overseas phone line.

Incorrect and inaccurate information:

— children may believe that everything they see on the internet is factual

— in fact, any person can put any information they like up on the internet and there is no guarantee that the information is accurate.

Inadvertently form 'friendships' with strangers: It is possible that children will come into contact with people who are pretending to be children but have other motives. There is a real danger that children may:

— come into contact with paedophiles

— provide personal details to strangers

— arrange to meet friends they have made on the internet without really knowing who they are

— be harassed by email.

Be subjected to advertising pressures: Once on the internet, children are likely to be subjected to unsolicited advertising. This could take the form of pop-up advertisements or ads embedded into particular websites. Such advertising often has bright colourful images and catchy phrases designed to put pressure on children to purchase goods on-line. A term for unsolicited advertising on the internet, the equivalent of junk mail in your letter box, is 'spam'.

Risk their personal health through excessive use: The internet can become addictive. It is important that children do not use the internet to the exclusion of other developmentally appropriate tasks including, the need to be physically active.

Endanger their privacy: Some sites encourage children to join clubs and enter competitions. In so doing, they reveal their name and address and may become the target of unwelcome marketing and other material.

Precautions to be taken by the Parents

There are several things that you can do to help counteract the dangers of the internet while allowing your children to use its benefits:

— learn more about it yourself

— be aware of what your children are doing on the internet

— establish guidelines about safe internet use

— teach your children to be critical users of the internet

— put in place reasonable boundaries

— use blocking software or filters

— if necessary, lodge complaints.

Learn more about it yourself: The more you know about the internet, the more support you will be able to provide your children. Many local libraries, schools and other community groups offer free courses or courses at reasonable prices. Don't forget, your children may be the best teaching resource you have — sit with them and ask them to help you understand. You don't have to become an expert, but some degree of comfort with the technology will help.

Be aware of what your children are doing on the internet: You can do this in a number of ways, including sitting with them while they are using the internet and chatting with them about what they are doing. You can also keep track of what is going on by:

— checking Bookmarks or Favorites (accessible via the icons on the menu bar) for sites your children like to visit often

— checking recently visited sites

— use monitoring software. One such product, released in 2003 is called SimGuard. This product enables parents to keep a record of a child's web browsing habits. The recommended way of using this software is to discuss its use with your children in the context of keeping them safe.

— email monitoring software is also available. KidSafe is an example of email monitoring software. It allows parents to filter email for their children to block out spam, viruses and offensive email.

Establish guidelines about safe internet use: There are several practical steps you can take to safeguard what happens in your home in respect of the internet:

- — keep the computer that is connected to the internet in a family area, not behind closed doors
- — only allow your children to use chat groups or news-groups or send email messages with your permission and under your supervision
- — talk to your children's school about their on-line policy; you may be able to put their safeguards into practice at home
- — select a reliable service provider and discuss children's on-line safety with them.

Teach children to be critical users of the internet: One of the best ways of protecting your children is to teach them to be critical users of the internet. Teach your children:

- — never to give others their name, the names of their friends, or fill in questionnaires with their personal details
- — never to send images of themselves over the net as they may be used for other purposes
- — about 'stranger danger' as it applies to the internet. If a child or young adult wishes to meet new on-line 'friends' in person, make sure you supervise the meeting.
- — never to respond to messages or bulletin board items that are suggestive, obscene, or threatening. Encourage your children to report such experiences to you. If they do, discuss these matters calmly with your child and forward a copy of any such messages to your service provider, asking for assistance.

— to only use monitored chat lines designed for their own age group

— to always be themselves when on-line

— to be critical in respect of 'information' found on the internet. Information on the internet comes from many sources and not all is reliable.

Use blocking software or filters: Blocking software or filters are the names used for programs that you can install and use on your computer to control the information that is accessed by children whilst on the internet. Blocking software:

— can block or minimise the risks of harmful violent material, sexually explicit material and chat lines being displayed on your computer

— is inexpensive and available from most computer suppliers or straight from the provider's sites

Whilst blocking software is an excellent idea for some age groups it is not foolproof and some computer aware children can still get around these programs. Blocking software goes hand in hand with parental supervision and is no substitute for it.

Put in place reasonable boundaries: Discuss with your children what you consider to be reasonable boundaries on use of the internet. Depending on the age of your child, negotiate these boundaries with them. For example: Set a daily or weekly time limit. The amount of time you decide upon will depend on the age and developmental stage of your child. Remember that the internet can be addictive and that you may need to encourage your child to keep a balance with other activities, including being physically active.

Only allow internet access in public spaces so that you can keep an eye on what they are accessing and discuss it with them if necessary Make it clear to them what materials are unacceptable. Make rules about on-line shopping, downloading material, responding to unsolicited advertisements and so on.

How much time should the child spend on the Internet

The Internet is a very useful tool for finding information, for contacting friends by email, and for chatting to others with similar interests. However, the Internet is but one means of communication, and one source of information among many. This topic outlines a few issues of a general nature that parents and caregivers may like to consider:

— the child's age and developmental needs

— reliability of information accessed

— safety considerations

— need for children to be physically active.

The child's age and developmental needs

— the greatest developmental need for children is to develop caring relationships with others

— it is also important to develop a good understanding of the way their community works and what it has to offer them.

Reliability of information accessed

— the information collected from the Internet may not always be reliable. The source of the information always needs to be checked.

— the local public library may be a better and more reliable source of information. It offers many things besides information, including contact with real people with many skills to offer.

Safety considerations

The Internet is not a safe place for children to play unsupervised. Their time with the Internet should be dependent on your ability and availability to provide supervision.

Need for children to be physically active

Time with the computers limit the opportunities for your child to be physically active. Extended periods of time at the screen, can lead to eyestrain, repetitive stress injuries, obesity and social isolation. Children's time with screen based media (including TV and computers) needs to be kept in balance with time in the real world with real people. For those in early childhood (under seven or eight) up to an hour a day is appropriate, and up to one and a half to 2 hours for older children.

Risks involved with the child using the Internet

The Internet links computers and databases world wide. It provides a most valuable communication system for obtaining information, sending mail, and chatting with others with similar interests. However, it is an adult world, and as such it can be a dangerous place for children to play because they may:

— inadvertently access inappropriate information

— come into contact with paedophiles

— be subjected to invasion of privacy and unsolicited advertising

— run the risk of becoming addicted

Inadvertently access inappropriate information:

— there are almost no restrictions on what can be placed on the world wide web

— there is no system of classification or age restrictions for accessing the Internet as there are for TV and films.

— it is not always easy to identify the source of the communication

— chat rooms can be full of strangers who use language which makes children and parents feel uncomfortable. There may be discussions on subjects that are inappropriate for a child to 'listen in on'. People may not be who they say they are.

— there is abundant material on the Internet that is sadistic and violent, or sexually explicit, and which can be damaging to children and young people's development. Such sites can easily be found accidentally. Some of it can appear superficially harmless and amusing.

— there are sites that provide information on criminal activity such as bomb making and drug abuse.

Come into contact with paedophiles:

— paedophiles use the Internet as a way of winning the trust of children and setting up meetings

— they also share information with each other on vulnerable children and how they can be approached.

Be subjected to invasion of privacy and unsolicited advertising:

— some commercial websites invade children's privacy by seeking personal information

— some sites offer and encourage children to acquire products or seek experiences which are costly and which many parents would consider unsuitable

— children may be encouraged to complete questionnaires and enter competitions that lead them to divulge personal information or incur unforeseen costs.

Run the risk of becoming addicted children and young people can become addicted and so absorbed in what cyberspace has to offer that little or no time is left for relating to people in person, or getting sufficient physical exercise

Internet filtering software

The Internet is a most valuable communication system for obtaining information, sending mail, and chatting with others with similar interests. However, there are risks with using the Internet. Some parents may wish to consider Internet filtering software as a method of reducing the risks of their children being exposed to undesirable material on the Internet.

There are a number of Internet filtering tools that parents can use. However, such tools are not infallible, and must be supplemented by parental vigilance. This is most easily achieved when children use a web-connected computer in the family room, and not in their private space. The three most commonly used varieties of Internet filtering software are filters, labels and safe zones.

Filters are software programs that can be put on your own computer, or can be made available through your Internet Service Provider (ISP). They :

— block access to web sites, based either on a list of banned sites, or on keywords or phrases.

— can stop search engines from searching for unsuitable topics

— may block access to newsgroups, chatrooms and email

— some can be set to control how much time your child spends on-line

— some offer the ability to shut down if certain sites are accessed.

Some methods used by filtering software are:

— a "black list"-keeps a list of blocked sites and allows access to all other sites

— a "white list"-keeps a list of sites that it is OK to view

— category blocking-groups sites into categories, and allows access or blocks according to the category (pornography, violence etc)

— graphics filters-block images, often relate to skin tones

— application blocking-allows or prevents access to specific applications such as chat rooms etc

— word and phrase blocking-prevents specific words or phrases being viewed

Labels: These tools attach labels to Internet sites. Your browser can be set to read the labels and block access to certain web sites. However, most web sites are unlabelled.

Safe zones: These are secure networks suitable for younger children, and are separate from the rest of the Internet. They are usually available only by subscription, or via some Internet Service Providers (ISPs).

Tips for parents in choosing filters

The following tips will guide parents' choice in filtering tools:

— for preschool children, consider using safe zones and other good sites that you select

— for children under 7 years, use a filtering tool that blocks access to newsgroups and chat rooms

— for older children, consider tools that filter access to chat rooms, and prevent them giving out personal information

— new Internet users should consider choosing easy to install tools that provide automatic free updates on lists of blocked sites

— examine what sort of material the tool covers and the options allowed for you to adjust what is blocked

— consider how often lists of blocked sites are updated and whether updates are free and automatic

Should the child have Internet access in his or her bedroom

The Internet is an adult medium, with little or no restriction on what is placed on it. On the positive side children can find useful information sources, fun computer games and entertaining web sites. However, they may also be exposed to exploitative commercial sites aimed at children and pornography networks. For this reason, children's access to the Internet must be supervised by their parents or caregivers. Filtering software can provide some help, but cannot replace the need for supervision.

Twelve tips for safe Internet use

— Spend some time with your child enjoying the exciting things on the Internet and discuss the ways they can use the internet for education and fun.

— Information on the Internet comes from many sources. Not all is reliable. Encourage a careful approach to 'information' found on the Internet.

— Be aware of what your children are doing on-line. Have the computer in a public area in the home, not in a bedroom or children's playroom.

— Encourage children to tell you about anything that worries them and have family talks about the dangers of the Internet.

— The Internet is fun, but full of strangers. Children should never give out personal information such as names and addresses.

— Many Internet sites have questionnaires and competitions. Ask your children to talk to you before filling in any forms.

— The Internet is a great place to make friends. However, not every one is who they seem to be. Children and young people should check with their parents before arranging any face to face meetings, and ensure that such meetings are in a public place, with an adult present.

— Encourage children to send e-mail only to friends, so they will have no need to correspond with strangers.

— Some information on chat lines is not appropriate for children. Teach them to say 'No' to messages, or to leave a site that makes them feel uncomfortable.

— If your child brings something inappropriate to your attention, tell them you are pleased they did and discuss it calmly.

— Encourage your child's school to develop a CyberSafety policy too.

— Too much time sitting at a computer can be unhealthy. Extensive use can result in repetitive stress injuries, eyestrain, obesity, and social isolation. Set a limit (an hour at most) and encourage your child to get out and explore the real world too.

Children's Internet Protection Act

The explosive growth of Internet use fueled in part by children's and teenagers' online activities. Children and teenagers use computers and the Internet more than any other age group. Access to the resources of the Internet has given children new research tools, information sources, avenues of expression, collaborative learning opportunities, and connections to other communities, among other benefits. But it also has potentially exposed them to the unseemly side of the Internet - indecent material, pornography, hate sites, violent sites, and online predators.

In USA, the National Academies released a report *in* August 2002 —*Youth, Pornography, and the Internet*— that studied tools and strategies for protecting children from online pornography. The report concluded that there are no "foreseeable technological 'silver bullets' or single permanent solutions" to keeping children safe from such material. Rather, the report supported solutions that balance the potential benefits of the Internet to children with the competing goals and values of the community.

As the dangers to children in an online environment have emerged, so have a variety of technology tools. Some common technologies used to protect children include:

— Filtering with Yes or No lists:

— *Server-side filtering:* Internet service providers and online server software offer filtering techniques to clients that deny access to particular content sources that have been pre-selected for blocking via automated processes, human review, and/or user options. The list of blocked URLs may or may not be disclosed and is regularly updated at the server level.

— *Client-side filtering:* This technology prohibits the browser from downloading content based on specified content sources identified by the user. Blocked sites may originate from both the software supplier and/or from the user's decision. Users maintain control over these lists with a password and may periodically download updated lists from the software's website. Some software filters out email or instant messaging.

— *Filtering using text-based content analysis:* This technology combines PC-based software and server software to conduct real time analysis of a website's content to filter out illicit content. Some software analyzes email and attachments. The user may or may not gain access to how such content is excluded.

— *Monitoring and time-limiting technologies:* This technology tracks a child's online activities and sets limits on the amount of time a child may spend online. Monitoring software often covers the Internet, email, and instant messaging activities.

— *Age Verification System:* This technology uses an independently-issued ID and controls the flow of online content by conditioning access to a web page with use of a password issued (by a third party) to an adult.

Even the most sophisticated and current technology tools are not one hundred percent effective. Public awareness campaigns and workshops have sought to supplement technology tools.

In 1996, the US Congress first attempted to curb inappropriate online content by passing the Communications Decency Act (CDA). The CDA prohibited the sending or posting of obscene or indecent material via the Internet to persons under the age of 18. The Supreme Court declared the law unconstitutional, however, stating that the law violated free speech under the First Amendment. Specifically, the Court ruled that CDA's vague provisions chilled free speech unknown to the speaker generating the content, and that the CDA's provisions criminalized legitimate, protected speech, including sexually explicit indecent speech, in addition to unprotected obscene speech.

Congress responded by passing the Child Online Protection Act (COPA) of 1998, a law written more narrowly to protect children from inappropriate online content. COPA prohibited commercial web sites from displaying "harmful to minors" material and imposed criminal penalties on violators. A three-judge panel for the United States District Court for the Eastern District of Pennsylvania ruled that COPA's reference to "contemporary community standards" violated the First Amendment when applied to the World Wide Web, and imposed an injunction on the enforcement of COPA. The Third Circuit affirmed this decision stating that the reference to community standards in the definition of "material that is harmful to minors" resulted in an overbroad statute. In May 2002, the Supreme Court vacated the Third Circuit decision and remanded the case for further review. The Court found that "contemporary community standards" by itself does not render the statute overbroad for purposes of the First Amendment. On remand, the Third Circuit found that COPA is not sufficiently narrowly tailored to satisfy the First Amendment requirements.

In October 2000, Congress passed the Children's Internet Protection Act (CIPA) of 2000. The law conditions the receipt of certain federal funding on educational institutions' adoption of technological protections and Internet safety policies. Sections 1712 and 1721 of CIPA, involving the use of filtered Internet access on public computers in libraries, were challenged in court as unconstitutional.

In May 2002, the United States District Court for the Eastern District of Pennsylvania struck down these provisions of CIPA as unconstitutional, stating that a technology's tendency to overblock material prohibits the flow of protected speech to library patrons. Under a provision within CIPA, providing for a fast-track appeals process requiring any appeals to be heard by the Supreme Court, the Justice Department appealed the court's decision to the Supreme Court. The Court agreed to review CIPA and heard oral arguments in March 2003.

In a plurality decision, the Supreme Court reversed the District Court's decision in June 2003, finding that the filtering provisions did not violate the First Amendment. Four justices held that (1) the Internet access provided by libraries is not a public forum, and therefore, decisions to block pornography are not subject to heightened scrutiny; (2) the disabling provision eases fears of "overblocking;" and (3) requiring filtering and blocking technology is an appropriate condition on the receipt of federal funding because libraries already exclude pornographic material from their other collections. The Supreme Court underscored "the ease with which patrons may have the filtering software disabled." The Federal Communications Commission subsequently issued an order to ensure that its implementation of CIPA complies with the Supreme Court's decision.

Evaluation of Existing Protection Measures

Section 1703(a) of CIPA requests National Telecommunications and Information Administration (NTIA) to initiate a notice and comment proceeding to determine whether currently available blocking and filtering technologies adequately address the needs of educational institutions, to make recommendations on how to foster the development of technologies that meet the needs of schools and libraries, and to evaluate current Internet safety policies. Section 1703(a) of CIPA specifically provides the following:

Sec. 1703. Study of Technology Protection Measures

a) IN GENERAL. Not later than 18 months after the date of the enactment of this Act, the National Telecommunications and Information Administration shall initiate a notice and comment proceeding for purposes of :

1) evaluating whether or not currently available technology protection measures, including commercial Internet blocking and filtering software, adequately address the needs of educational institutions;

2) making recommendations on how to foster the development of measures that meet such needs; and

3) evaluating the development and effectiveness of local Internet safety policies that are currently in operation after community input.

On May 24, 2002, NTIA published a "Request for Comment" in the Federal Register, eliciting information about technology protection measures and Internet safety policies. NTIA requested interested parties to submit written comments on any issue of fact, law, or policy germane to the evaluation. NTIA also encouraged commenters to submit copies of relevant studies, surveys, research, or other empirical data. NTIA did not seek comment on the constitutionality of the statute or its provisions. In order to generate a wide range of responses, NTIA conducted extensive outreach to the education community, technology developers, consumer groups, and academia. The "Request for Comment" elicited 42 comments from associations, technology vendors, governmental agencies, academics/university professors, schools, and libraries.

Section 1703 of CIPA requests that NTIA evaluate whether currently available technology protection measures, including commercial Internet blocking and filtering software, adequately address the needs of educational institutions. In answering this inquiry, the commenters identified six needs of educational institutions:

1) balancing the importance of allowing children to use the Internet with the importance of protecting children from inappropriate material;
2) accessing online educational materials with a minimum level of relevant content being blocked;
3) deciding on the local level how best to protect children from Internet dangers;
4) understanding how to fully utilize Internet protection technology measures;
5) considering a variety of technical, educational, and economic factors when selecting technology protection measures; and
6) adopting an Internet safety strategy that includes technology, human monitoring, and education.

Below we examine these needs and set forth the commenters' evaluation of whether existing technology protection measures are meeting each of these needs.

Balancing the Importance of Allowing Children to Use the Internet with the Importance of Protecting Children From Inappropriate Material

Congress passed CIPA to protect children from inappropriate and harmful content while accessing the Internet at educational institutions that use federal funds. Commenters expressed little doubt that technology plays a role in reducing a child's exposure to inappropriate content. Many commenters wrote of their use of technology protection measures. Several comments from schools and libraries reported using Internet-content filters in order to assist in a safer Internet experience. Some institutions install filters specifically on Internet stations for children under eighteen. Some schools reported the effective use of filtering software. For example, St. Pius X School in Urbandale, Iowa reported using firewall filtering as well as customizable blocking to meet its protection needs. The school's administrators select sites and domains to block with the option to "unlock" those sites at a later time. One public library described filters as "easy to use," giving students "access to most sites they need in school." The library also reported few, if any, problems associated with filtered Internet use.

NTIA also received comments that referenced the results of 26 independent laboratory tests on filters conducted between 1995 and 2001 by ten professional testing laboratories. The labs conducted 108 individual product tests examining filtering software. The test results grouped products into three categories: "found filters effective," "found filters of mixed effectiveness," and "found filters ineffective." Nineteen of the twenty-six product tests found filters effective, four product tests found filters of mixed effectiveness, and three product tests found filters ineffective. Based on these results, the commenters that drew NTIA's attention to this study concluded that filtering is an effective method of protecting children from inappropriate material.

Where filtering fell short of being effective, the situation usually involved either overblocking or underblocking of material. Numerous commenters discussed the effect of overblocking and underblocking of online content as it relates to the needs of educational institutions. The United States District Court for the

Eastern District of Pennsylvania defined overblocking as, "the blocking of content that does not meet the category definitions established by CIPA or by the filtering software companies," and underblocking as "leaving off of a control list a URL that contains content that would meet the category definitions defined by CIPA or the filtering software companies."

One concern resulting from overblocking is the restricted ability of users to view appropriate content and legitimate online research. Comments from the education community acknowledged that despite training and education, technology still fails to meet the needs of educators by missing inappropriate sites, or by depriving students and teachers of access to legitimate information. Two commenters expressed particular concern with the latter situation. A study by the Pew Internet and American Life Project recently found that: "[w]hile many students recognize the need to shelter teenagers from inappropriate material and adult-oriented commercial ads, they complain that blocking and filtering software often raises barriers to students' legitimate educational use of the Internet. Most of our students feel that filtering software blocks important information, and many feel discouraged from using the Internet by the difficulties they face in accessing educational material."

Other comments referred to the United States District Court for the Eastern District of Pennsylvania's May 24, 2002 decision declaring CIPA Sections 1712 and Section 1721 facially invalid under the First Amendment. A three-judge panel convened an eight-day trial to decide the issues related to the effectiveness of currently available technology protection measures. The commenters directed NTIA's attention to the court's discussion of the difficulties with the Internet's structural composition that impinge upon the filtering software's ability to block content effectively.

The court described the Internet as a decentralized, interconnected network with millions of web pages linked to thousands of additional web pages to create the "publicly indexable web." These links enable search engines to sort and index material by following links from one web page to another. Accordingly, search engines often fail to categorize isolated web pages not connected by these links. Witness testimony estimated that fifty percent of the Internet currently remains incapable of being indexed, thereby further invalidating the effectiveness of filtering technologies.

The court heard testimony from three leading filtering companies who explained the methods used to filter content. Typically, filtering software products separate appropriate and inappropriate content by compiling category lists such as: adult/sexually explicit, arts, alcohol, business, chat, dating, education, entertainment, hate speech, health, illegal, news, religion, and violence. Users determine which content to block by selecting from pre-determined category lists.

Additional testimony was to the effect that the filtering technologies are incapable of effectively blocking the majority of content defined by CIPA without also blocking a substantial amount of protected speech. As indicated by government witnesses, every filtering software product demonstrated excluded between 6 percent and 15 percent of protected speech. The court evaluated why filtering software overblocked or underblocked material and concluded that: filtering companies focus on reviewing fresh content or newly posted web addresses and spend little time on reviewing the accuracy of websites previously categorized; inconsistencies exist between filtering definitions for pornography and CIPA's legal definitions of obscenity, child pornography, or content harmful to minors; community standards vary with regard to categorizing content; and the available technology is generally unable to meet CIPA's requirement that filters block visual depictions, but not text.

Based on the comments, existing technology protection measures are helping to meet the concerns of educational institutions to protect children from inappropriate materials they may encounter while using the Internet. The occurrence of overblocking and underblocking, however, has resulted in some dissatisfaction and frustration by users with the existing technology protection measures.

Accessing Online Educational Materials with a Minimum Level of Relevant Content Being Blocked

While existing technology protection measures, such as filtering software, are able to block much of which is deemed inappropriate material for children, the technology measures also sometimes block online educational content sought by teachers. Commenters from both individual schools and associations representing schools discussed the difficulties that educators experience when planning lessons based on online content.

The Consortium for School Networking (COSN) polled their members and found that filtering and blocking technologies often block lessons planned by teachers from home, including educational websites. For example, this experience caused frustration for a program in Missouri that furnishes teachers with laptops for the specific purpose of preparing lessons at home. The technology in these schools often blocks access to web sites pre-selected by teachers. Teachers in these schools usually discover the blocked web sites during a lesson, forcing them to react quickly and find new, suitable content.

One response to this situation is the COSN's June 2001 report, "Safeguarding the Wired Schoolhouse," which provides guidance to educators using the Internet to supplement their lessons with educational content and resources that evaluate web sites, search strategies, search engines, and web lessons. Two examples provided in the report include the Montgomery County Public Schools' and the Washington Library Media Assrciation's development of websites about information literacy and the creation of web lessons.

Congress included several "disabling provisions" within CIPA allowing administrators to disable technology for certain bona fide research or other lawful purposes. Although some claim that Congress intended these provisions to cure the overblocking tendencies of technology protection measures, some commenters expressed concern that the provisions affect differently those recipients receiving E-rate funds and those receiving Department of Education funds. For example, the recipients of Department of Education funds may "disable for certain use" and recipients of E-rate funds may "disable during adult use." The comments further explained that "disabling for certain use" permits administrators to supersede technology for both adults and students, whereas "disabling during adult use," limits a school's flexibility to supersede technology.

Some schools noted that by creating different standards based on the source of federal funds, these provisions generate confusion and reluctance within educational communities about using disabling technology to accommodate override requests for fear of breaching CIPA. Some commenters perceived the override provision as failing to cure the overblocking concerns when educators or students desire immediate access to educationally-related material.

Based on the comments, some educators are having difficulties with existing technology protection measures in meeting their need to be able to access online educational materials with a minimum level of relevant content being blocked. The disabling provisions of CIPA do not appear to be a satisfactory answer for some educators.

Deciding on the Local Level How Best to Protect Children from Internet Dangers.

Several commenters stated that CIPA's provisions requiring educational institutions to install technology protection measures on computers removes local decision making from educators. Comments from associations representing schools explained that schools often adopt locally-based Internet solutions reflecting the unique circumstances of the community, such as: faculty and staff familiarity with technology; level of patron and parental involvement; values of the community; funding resources; size of the community and educational institution; degree of supervision; education philosophy; and political will of library and school board members. Further, schools prefer making decisions locally to reflect local resources (financial and human), values, and community concerns.

Commenters also tended to disagree regarding the access to selection criteria developed by software companies for filtering products. For example, educators argue that, without an understanding of how technology companies select blocking criteria, educators possibly subject themselves to non-educational standards and the ideas and policies of outside parties. Yet, according to the comments submitted by a technology developer of blocking and filtering software, the company provides extensive information to users and publishes details about the categories of sites it blocks.

Several vendors' comments discussed their products' ability to allow users to type in a web address to learn more about a particular site's blocking category. Additionally, one vendor discussed its efforts to seek user feedback and to respond promptly to consumer requests to add, delete, or change a blocked web site. To that end, the company received over 60,000 requests between January 1, 2002 and August 15, 2002, and reviewed each request within two days. Of these requests, twenty percent resulted in an addition, deletion or change. On the other hand, two commenters noted that many technology companies choose not to release their blocked lists for a variety of reasons including: the list's proprietary nature and source code; the risk of abuse by competitors; the expense associated with a carefully created database; the harmful effect to children; the diminished value of a published list; and the general privacy policy of the company. In addition, the National Education Association's comments stated that, generally, category descriptions vary in scope, detail, and helpfulness. One advocacy group claimed that the employees of filtering companies may apply their own subjective judgments or reflect the manufacturers' social and political views when reviewing content web sites.

In addition to preferring that technology companies release their lists of blocked sites, educational institutions questioned the process filtering companies use to develop and define blocking criteria. The American Library Association expressed uneasiness with selecting technology tools to accommodate the wide-ranging values of their patrons when most libraries feel uncertainty about the blocking decisions made by companies. The Center for Democracy and Technology agreed that technology users enjoy little input into blocking decisions, noting that, "in designing filtering tools, companies seek to meet the needs of diverse consumer groups and thus intentionally choose to block sites that may be undesirable or offensive to a particular audience or targeted consumer group but deemed appropriate by another."

Many commenters cited to the U.S. District Court decision to highlight the desire of educational institutions to make decisions locally, and the need to understand categories pre-selected by filtering companies. Additionally, commenters discussed that the blocking categories defined by filtering companies rarely correspond with CIPA's definition and these categories cannot be customized to comply with CIPA. The comments underscored in a number of ways the belief by some educational institutions that existing technology measures fell short of meeting their need to decide locally how to protect the children in their community from Internet dangers.

Understanding How to Fully Utilize Internet Protection Technology Measures

The comments indicated that educators need training to fully understand how to use the technology protection measures in order to accommodate bona fide and other lawful research, as well as to meet other needs of their specific environment. Several comments noted the difficulty of adjusting a technology tool to override a blocked web site. Many commenters acknowledged that overblocking of helpful educational material occurs with many filtering products and, consequently, teachers need training on how to disable filtering software for minors conducting educational searches or other legitimate research.

The commenters also noted instances where educators experienced delays with an override. The Consortium of School Networking (COSN) asked their members to report their experience with override requests. They found that the time it took to request an override and receive a response ranged from less than five minutes to as long as one week. Some institutions lacked an override policy altogether. One association's comments summarized the end result of these issues as extremely frustrating for teachers who lack training on how to disable filtering technology.

NTIA also received a variety of responses discussing educators' experience with adjusting technology protection measures to accommodate all age groups and grades. The comments indicate the need for training educators on how to adjust technology protection measures to accommodate different age groups. One commenter stated that its filtering technology does not adjust blocking content based on the age of the child. Yet, many technology products offer users the ability to customize. One technology vendor provided NTIA with an example of its product's web site customization feature. Specifically, the product gives the user the ability to add sites to a block list. Another commenter described a software program that accommodates six age groups: unfiltered access-adults; teen access-15 to 17; pre-teen-12 to 14; kid-8 to 11; child-7 & under. While many products exist that adjust to different ages, some commenters disagreed with the effectiveness or ease of adjusting the technology to accommodate various ages or grades. One commenter noted that relying on age specific categories works well for younger children, but varying maturity levels makes it more difficult to cluster older children by age and rely upon the categories pre-selected by technology vendors.

Based on the comments, existing technology protection measures are capable of meeting a number of the needs of educational institutions. However, some educators are unaware of the capabilities of these measures or lack the knowledge about how to use many features of the technology protection tools.

Considering a Variety of Technical, Educational, and Economic Factors When Selecting Technology Protection Measures

Commenters listed several factors that educational institutions take into account prior to selecting technology. Most commenters cited cost as the primary factor. One commenter mentioned that when institutions consider cost, they often choose cheaper and less sophisticated products. Schools and libraries also noted that they obtain very little extra funding to pay for Internet protection measures. The E-Rate program, which gives schools and libraries discounts on telephone service, Internet access, and internal connections, does not cover technology protection measures, such as filtering and blocking software. In addition to cost, comments from educational associations listed maintenance, effectiveness, ability to customize, network impact, and upgrades as important factors considered when selecting technology protection measures. In sum, the commenters noted that educational institutions consider a variety of economic, technical, and educational factors when selecting technology protection measures.

Adopting an Internet Safety Strategy that Includes Technology, Human Monitoring, and Education

Commenters responding to NTIA's Request for Comment described their experience with the use of technology protection measures within educational institutions. Many educational institutions discussed their use of filtering and blocking technology to protect children from inappropriate content. Others explained their use of a combination of technology and non-technical protection strategies, such as human monitoring or Internet safety policies, to achieve this goal.

Interestingly, the comments revealed that the measures adopted by educational institutions depend in part on their interpretation of CIPA. One commenter noted that educational institutions trying to comply with CIPA interpret the language "technology protection measures" as a requirement to install only filtering software, and often do not explore other technical remedies. This commenter also stated that many educational institutions interpret CIPA's "technology protection measure" language as limited to "commercial, proprietary-protected filtering software."

A trade association noted that this narrow interpretation of CIPA's technology protection measure requirement may inhibit schools and libraries from adopting more comprehensive solutions that encompass both technology and education. Some commenters did discuss other technology measures, such as monitoring software, but there were no comments from educational institutions regarding their experience as users of monitoring software.

The Federal Communications Commission's (FCC) rules interpret CIPA as encouraging educational institutions to adopt both technological and non-technological measures to protect children online. FCC regulations require schools and libraries to certify that they have adopted:

— An Internet safety policy that blocks and filters certain visual depictions for both minors and adults;

— An Internet safety policy that includes monitoring;

— An Internet safety policy that addresses: access to inappropriate material; email, chat, and other forms of electronic communications; hacking; disclosure of a minor's personal information; and measures restricting material that is harmful to minors.

A report released in September 2002 by the U.S. Department of Education's National Center for Educational Statistics supports the conclusion that educational institutions rely on a combination approach to shield children from inappropriate online content. The report documents that, in 2001, 96 percent of public schools used a variety of technologies or policies to protect children from inappropriate content. Of these schools, 91 percent relied on teacher or staff monitoring; 87 percent installed blocking or filtering software; 80 percent required parents to sign a written contract; 75 percent required students to sign a written contract; 44 percent adopted an honor code; and 26 percent confined school access to an intranet.

Notwithstanding some commenters' interpretation of CIPA, the majority of comments indicated that most educational institutions prefer a combination of technology and education to ensure a safe online environment. Members of the International Society of Technology in Education (ISTE) adopted numerous methods to ensure that students had a safe, educational, and age appropriate experience online, including acceptable use policies, software technologies, teacher monitoring and supervision, and student education programs. A trade association representing schools stated that most educational institutions adopt diverse Internet protection solutions that correspond with the culture and resources of their community.

Several commenters indicated a preference for non-technological solutions or a need to supplement technology with non-technical measures to create a safe online environment. For example, the State Education Department of the University of the State of New York relies on broadly written acceptable use policies as their protection method of choice. It views technology-based solutions as geared toward content issues only, leaving the other challenges associated with public Internet access unaddressed. Thus, it adopted written policies to manage a wide-range of additional specific behaviors, such as patron access, noise levels, and computer tampering.

A school in Albuquerque, New Mexico, took a different approach. As an individual serving as a volunteer school technology coordinator explained, the school adopted student monitoring and pre-selected sites over filtering technology, not only because of the unreliability of technology and the cost, but also because of an inadequate budget to train staff. This commenter concludes that the creation of "yes" lists, or pre-selected child-appropriate content, serves to keep children protected from harmful content.

Some libraries are also emphasizing a non-technical approach to safeguarding children from harmful content. The Board of the Evanston Public Library in Illinois implemented a library use policy instead of filtering software for its computers. The policy encourages parents to accompany their children and supervise their Internet access. Additionally, librarians configure children's computers for "focused Internet access," directing kids to pre-select age-appropriate websites.

The Charles M. Bailey Public Library in Winthrop, Maine utilizes a combination of bookmarks, web design, parental involvement, and technology education classes for children to create a safe online environment. The Las Vegas Clark County Library District (LVCCLD) uses an approach giving patrons numerous options to protect themselves online. The library prefers an "empowerment" approach offering patrons the choice to control their Internet access level with various educational and informational methods.

Based on the comments, existing technology protection measures are capable of meeting the technology component of an approach that includes both technology and non-technical protection strategies.

In sum, NTIA gleaned six distinct needs within educational institutions:

(1) balancing the importance of allowing children to use the Internet with the importance of protecting children from inappropriate material;

(2) accessing online educational materials with a minimum level of relevant content being blocked;

(3) deciding locally how best to protect children from Internet dangers;

(4) understanding how to fully utilize Internet protection technology measures;

(5) considering a variety of technical, educational, and economic factors when selecting technology protection measures; and

(6) adopting an Internet safety strategy that includes technology, human monitoring, and education.

As articulated in the comments, existing technology protection measures, by themselves, are meeting most, but not all, of these needs. Below we discuss ways to foster the development of measures that would more fully meet these needs of educational institutions.

Fostering the Development of Measures that Meet the Needs of Educational Institutions

NTIA found that educational institutions experienced frustration with the marketplace for not developing new and advanced technology protection measures. NTIA asked commenters to discuss the development of new technology features that would better meet the needs of educational institutions. NTIA received a variety of responses indicating that the following technology features would best assist educational institutions today.

— Technology that scans a website's content, rather than relying on key words;

— Customer access to lists of blocked sites by subject area;

— Individual logins to allow flexibility in grades kindergarten through 12 or child/adult settings;

— Ability of a system administrator or local technician to edit or override blocked sites in real time; and

— Image recognition technology.

Comments from four technology vendors explained how their technology blocks categorized content, and described features associated with their product. The vendors offer many of the features desired by the education community. For example:

DoBox described its technology as able to manage all facets of Internet access, including Web, email, chat/instant messaging, applications/games, and peer to peer systems. Its product allows local customization by user and by group, and allows authorized individuals to add immediately sites to be blocked or permit sites for permanent or temporary access.

Kidsnet described its product, EducationNet, as providing educators with three levels of protection:

1) relying on 100 percent human review of all web site content;
2) basing content review on transparent and adaptable criteria; and
3) adapting categories to fit various ages or levels and different needs of institutions.

N2H2 relies on a confidential and proprietary database of 42 categories, giving users the choice of any or all of these categories. N2H2 updates the database and creates a new version daily. N2H2 follows four steps to categorize sites:

(1) flag URLs for categorization; (2) match and flag URL for review; (3) examine and categorize; and (4) reexamine URLs in database. N2H2 also publicly releases details, descriptions, and criteria of the 42 content categories on their website.

The Vericept Corporation, formally known as E-sniff, combines URL filtering with "comprehensive content monitoring" for all forms of Internet access. Vericept described "comprehensive content monitoring" as tools that track all inappropriate content flowing through the network. Users determine "inappropriate" content based upon reports generated from network traffic.

Based on the four descriptions, these existing products offer features similar to those requested by educational institutions.

Through independent research, NTIA also found that more companies are increasingly entering the market for Internet content protection technology. Some analysts predict that the growth of the networking and protection market can be attributed to increased Internet access, the exponential growth of web pages, and the increasing desire of families, schools, and libraries to protect children from inappropriate content and interactions on the Internet. Some analysts predict that the market for these products will rise to over $600 million by 2004 at a rate of nearly 50 percent per year.

The more-established Internet content filtering companies appear to be increasing the amount of money that they put into their research and development divisions. Numerous venture capital firms invest in these Internet-safety technology companies as well, both within the United States and abroad. In addition to U.S.-made

Internet content filters, international companies are developing filtering software. Currently, over fifty companies exist that provide this technology. NTIA found that while a substantial number of technology companies exist that invest in the research and development of technology protection measures, educational institutions are either unaware of the diverse array of products available to meet their needs or lack the training to fully utilize the products.

Some commenters claim that CIPA locked in filtering and blocking technology as the "technology protection measure" of choice, thereby stifling potential innovation of technology protection measures. According to several commenters, little incentive exists for the markets to develop more flexible technology products to meet the needs of educational institutions if investors or venture capitalists perceive the education community as demanding only one type of technology. The Consortium for School Networking writes that CIPA "forced all of the companies competing in the market to define their product in terms of which best complies with CIPA, rather than how they may serve the needs of different kinds of school districts."

While some commenters encouraged technology vendors to develop new protection products to meet educators' needs, others believed that the focus of attention should not be on new technologies. Rather, they believe that the focus of attention should be on the development and implementation of a comprehensive education and supervision approach to protect children by preparing them to make safe and responsible choices.

NTIA Recommendations

Section 1703(a)(2) of CIPA invited NTIA to make any recommendations to Congress on how to foster the development of measures that meet the needs of educational institutions. Based on the comments, NTIA has identified two recommendations: (1) vendors should offer training services to educational institutions so the institutions can understand and use fully the capabilities of technology protection measures; and (2) Congress should amend CIPA's language to clarify the term "technology protection measures."

Training

The majority of comments from educational institutions noted that some educators often lack the training necessary to use fully the available technology tools. For example, although CIPA includes several provisions giving adults the authority to override technology for certain bona fide or other legitimate research, some educators often do not know how to disable the technology. Commenters also indicated their desire that software perform specific tasks, such as scanning content rather than relying on key words; listing blocked sites by subject area; allowing individual log-ins to accommodate varying ages; and allowing editing and overriding of blocked sites in real time. NTIA identified a disconnect between the specific needs listed by educational entities and the current capabilities of available technology. NTIA found that, while commenters discussed the desire for certain technological capabilities, the vendors' comments explained that their technology already performs many of these tasks.

NTIA recognizes that, as educational institutions become familiar with using technology protection measures, the need for training may decrease. Until that time, however, NTIA agrees with commenters who expressed the importance of training as part of the solution to protect children from illicit online content. NTIA suggests that as part of promotional efforts to advertise products or as part of the initial orientation to their products, technology vendors should train and educate teachers, administrative personnel, librarians, and other educational personnel on the specific features of their product.

Legislative Language

Commenters discussed the difficulty that some educational institutions have interpreting CIPA's "technology protection measure" language. Some commenters claim that many educational institutions default to "filtering" technology only, without researching other types of technology protection options. As a result, many believe that this reliance on mostly filtering products stifles the marketplace and serves as a disincentive for technology companies to invest in the research and development of newer and more sophisticated products. Moreover, as set forth above, filtering and blocking software has not been able to overcome problems of overblocking, inability to generate an updated index for the Internet, and lack of correspondence to statutory definitions and categories. Yet, other technology tools can or have the potential to address better the needs of educational institutions. Thus, NTIA recommends that Congress change the current legislation to clarify that the term "technology protection measure" encompasses not only filtering and blocking software, but also other current and future technology tools. Specifically, Section 1703(3) of CIPA currently reads as follows:

Technology Protection Measure

The term "technology protection measure" means a specific technology that blocks or filters Internet access to visual depictions that are—(a) obscene, as that term is defined in section 1460 of title 18, United States Code; (b) child pornography, as that term is defined in section 2256 of title 18, United States Code; or (c) harmful to minors.

NTIA recommends replacing the above language with the following:

> Technology Protection Measures - The term "technology protection measure" means a specific technology that prevents Internet access to visual depictions that are -- (a) obscene, as that term is defined in section 1460 of title 18, United States Code; (b) child pornography, as that term is defined in section 2256 of title 18, United States Code; or (c) harmful to minors.

NTIA believes this expanded definition using the word "prevents" will encourage educational institutions to utilize technology, in addition to blocking and filtering software, that may better meet their needs as outlined above. A wider selection of products should give local decision makers more options to find the products that best meet their community's needs.

Alternatively to amending CIPA, NTIA recommends that the FCC and the U.S. Department of Education (DOE) provide further guidance to recipients of E-rate or DOE funds on the meaning of technology protection measures.

Development of Internet Safety Policies

NTIA found that educational institutions have engaged in discussions with their respective communities to create acceptable Internet safety policies. Educational institutions tend to incorporate the values and needs of their community into their policy and, as a result, experience positive feedback about their policy's success as part of the solution to protect children online. Most of the commenters expressed a great deal of satisfaction with the evolution and use of safety policies and praised CIPA for giving educational institutions the autonomy to develop their own policies. The Consortium for School Networking (COSN) expressed appreciation that CIPA allowed schools to draft policies reflecting the needs of the community and school environment. The State Education Department of the University of the State of New York credits its safety policies as the most effective strategy employed to keep patrons in conformance with library rules. The policy's success begins with staff-wide understanding of the policy's content, followed by consistent application, on-going review, and community involvement.

Several public libraries post Internet safety policies that appear whenever a patron logs onto a public computer. In these instances, Internet access requires patrons to click an acceptance explaining his or her agreement and asks the individual to abide by the terms of the policy. The policy states that patrons may access constitutionally- protected online material, and that patrons may not use the Internet in an inappropriate manner for a public area. The policy also lists specific, prohibited behaviors, such as accessing obscene material, accessing materials harmful to minors, or engaging in offensive, intimidating, or hostile behavior. In the two years since implementing the policy, these librarians indicate that they have witnessed only a few instances of inappropriate patron behavior, and attribute their Internet safety policy with contributing to a trouble-free environment and creating a safe-online experience.

Educational institutions also consider Internet safety policies as an avenue to teach children about online safety skills. Some suggested important safety skills may include teaching children about taking appropriate actions when harmful content appears online; teaching children to report threatening/disturbing correspondence online; or arming children with strategies if approached by a stranger. Additionally, one commenter underscored that Internet safety policies must be reviewed regularly to guarantee that they adequately reflect the views of the community and cover the appropriate technology.

NTIA found that Internet safety policies are generally effective when educational institutions customize Internet safety policies to the needs of the community. Many communities opt to keep their policies flexible to adapt to evolving technologies and the changing needs of the community.

The National Research Council report studied Acceptable Use Policies, similar to the Internet safety policy. The report defined acceptable use policies as "a set of guidelines and expectations about how individuals will conduct themselves online." Accordingly, these policies make young people responsible for their online behavior and encourage personal accountability for responsible Internet use. The report endorses effective policies as including sanctions for violations; soliciting input from parents, community members, schools, libraries, and students; and using accidental violations as opportunities to educate users about how to avoid similar situations.

NTIA asked participants to discuss their experience with successful Internet safety approaches or "best practices." NTIA grouped the responses into the following categories: acceptable use policies, child media literacy, parental education and awareness, staff education and development, identification of appropriate content, and child-safe areas. A summary of successful best practices provided by the comments is detailed below:

Acceptable Use Policies

Post guidelines and consequences for Internet use: Ensure appropriate behavior through awareness of the policy guidelines and consequences, followed by consistent enforcement of the policy. Authorize staff to terminate Internet sessions for users who fail to comply with the policy.

On-screen Appropriate Use Policy: Require Internet users to agree to abide by these policies before gaining access to the Internet.

Age/Education criteria: Establish flexible policies that accommodate different ages and implement education settings with varying degrees of supervision.

Child Media Literacy

Internet safety courses: Teach students about how to use the Internet safely, report bad activity, ignore and report harassment or threats, protect their privacy and personal information, and detect information that is not appropriate.

Online safety videos: Provide students, parents, and teachers with a video teaching Internet safety and successful use skills.

Internet search skills: Teach students skills to conduct successful, safe Internet searches using keywords and search engines.

Learning to evaluate online material: Teach children to evaluate the veracity, appropriateness, and educational value of websites.

Internet drivers' licenses: Require students to take an Internet safety and use course, followed by a test that students must pass in order to receive the privilege of using the Internet at school.

Parental Education and Awareness

Educate families about technology and the Internet: Encourage parental involvement, as this often leads to safer online experiences for children.

Parental supervision: Rely not only on filters, but also on parental supervision as means of protecting children from harmful content. Encourage parents to pay attention to how and when students use the Internet, and to be responsive with intervention and discipline.

Staff Education and Development

Curriculum tailored sites: Educate teachers about how to find, bookmark, and provide for their students those web sites that complement safe teaching materials.

Teacher Training: Train teachers to effectively use technology.

Identification of Appropriate Content

Pre-approved hotlinks: Administrators and educators pre-select safe and appropriate sites for child access.

Teacher lessons: Teachers create lesson plans with laptops at home tailored to specific subject areas/ curriculum.

Creation of pre-approved "yes" lists: Allow access only to those sites that have been pre-approved as safe and appropriate.

Child-Safe Areas

Filtered: Designate a specific children's computer room with filters installed on the computers. Combine filtered access with Internet education and safety.

Children's monitors in public view: Discourage use policy violations by allowing others to see the monitors.

Enclosed Internet stations for adults: Screen adult workstations from child-safe areas.

NTIA asked commenters for lessons learned from their experience with Internet safety policies. One Internet safety expert told NTIA that in order to ensure successful policies governing children's Internet use, drafters of such policies should discuss the following: guidelines/purpose, sharing networks/resources, passwords, email, privacy, copyright and plagiarism, Internet access, and safety. Another group encouraged teachers and librarians to establish policies that: give educators autonomy for classroom curriculum materials; address the different ages of students and different educational settings (classroom use, library use, after school enrichment); and implement effective human and technical monitoring strategies. An education trade group wrote that Internet safety policies should not be regarded as "just another form for parental signature," but rather these policies must be given special status, and the policy's principles must be fully integrated into the school curriculum.

Other comments discussed the importance of incorporating clear violations and sanctions into safety policies. For example, a program in Missouri encourages strong consequences of computer misuse. If a student intentionally misuses the computer, the student forfeits all computer privileges and the school informs the student's parent of the violation. If a student unintentionally misuses the computer, the student must immediately turn off the computer and raise his or her hand for the teacher to handle the situation. The program praised this policy as keeping violations to a minimum largely due to the policy's clarity and consistent enforcement.

Commenters also noted several difficulties with employing technology without acceptable use policies to protect children. First, commenters noted that technology protection measures are not the entire answer. These commenters emphasized that technology protection measures are most effective when teachers and educational institutions can customize technology and use it in connection with other strategies and tools. As one commenter stated, children need to be trained to think critically and use the Internet safely. Technology cannot replace education and judgment. Second, one commenter noted that technology protection measures can give a false sense of protection. This commenter stated that children should be educated to avoid improper content in the same unfiltered environments children experience in their homes, libraries, and offices. He argued that filtering provides an inauthentic atmosphere that thwarts teachers' preparing their students to deal with reality. Alternatively, another commenter argued that acceptable use policies may give a false sense of protection. The commenter noted that appropriate use policies are a good protection measure, but there is an assumption that children can avoid offensive material simply by education. He also contended that time limits imposed by acceptable use policies have not been found to stop the ability of children to access inappropriate material online.

Another difficulty that commenters highlighted is the constraints of the school environment. They noted that the classroom setting is not always amenable to monitoring. They also stated that teachers express uncertainty about their role as monitor watching children online. They noted that some teachers lack the requisite knowledge and sophistication about technology.

The National Research Council report also discussed several issues relating to acceptable use policies. The Council recommended that these policies should: distinguish between adult and child use; distinguish between younger and older children; determine how to measure compliance; avoid overly broad wording and strive to list specific inappropriate behavior and material; protect against liability; and define a user's rights.

The best practices and lessons learned that are set forth above provide valuable information for communities to consider as they develop and implement Internet safety policies.

In sum, existing technology protection measures have met many of the needs of educational institutions. While the education community has had success with technology measures, however, the education community also recognizes that comprehensive child protection solutions do not rest solely with technology.

Technology protection measures are most effective when teachers and educational institutions can customize technology and use it in connection with other strategies and tools. Educational institutions prefer local decision making that gives leaders the flexibility to select the appropriate technology that fits best with their unique circumstances and to consider non-economic factors that may influence technology selection decisions.

6

Regulation of Violent Entertainment

Given the evidence that violent materials in television, films, music, video games, and the Internet have harmful effects, we must be concerned about how, and to what extent, these materials are marketed, sold, and otherwise made available to children. The evidence is not encouraging. Any frequent visitor to a movie theater could confirm that theater personnel are less than diligent in preventing juveniles from viewing R-rated movies. And for many of these films, such as "teen-slasher" hits "Scream," "Disturbing Behavior," and "I Know What You Did Last Summer," America's youth are in fact the target audience.

The story is maddeningly similar for video games, the Internet, and music. In US, the National Institute on Media and Family found that, despite the rating system in place for video games, in 1998, only 21% of retail and rental stores had any policies prohibiting the sale or rental of adult games to minors. Earlier this year the Senate Commerce Committee heard testimony about a 12-year-old boy who bought the video games "Doom" and "Quake"--both of which are rated for adults only--at a

Washington, D.C. video store at the recommendation of the store clerk. The National Institute on Media and the Family also found that some manufacturers of video games are marketing to children ultra-violent products rated only for adults. One such video game, "Resident Evil 2," was advertised in the magazine "Sports Illustrated for Kids."

As for the Internet, there are thousands of websites celebrating hate, racism, extremism, and violence. One such site is operated by the notorious World Church of the Creator, which claims to be "established for the survival, expansion and advancement of our white race exclusively," and is engaged in a struggle against the "Jewish occupational Government of the United States." In the past several months several hate crimes (including multiple) murders have been linked to adherents of this "church." Some websites also offer versions of popular video games illegally altered to promote racism and violence. For example, the game "White Power Doom," adapted from the game "Doom," promotes a neo-Nazi agenda; another such game, "White Power Wolfenstein," is replete with Nazi symbols and imagery of the Holocaust. Without filtering/blocking technology and a rating system, such websites can be explored by anyone with a computer and access to the Internet, including children.

The Entertainment Software Rating Board (ESRB) has developed a promising voluntary rating system for Internet material, for which they should be commended. Unfortunately, the effectiveness of the system has been undermined by the unwillingness of website operators to submit information about their sites to the ESRB. Finally, with respect to music, the labeling program is voluntary, and many retailers simply choose not to restrict purchasing by minors. It was hardly surprising, then, when the Senate Commerce Committee heard how the same 12-year-old who purchased adult-only video games bought a Marilyn Manson compact disc from a Washington, D.C. record store. Ironically, the warning label on the disc was covered by the price tag.

Former United States Senator Paul Simon observed several years ago that "Thirty seconds of a soap bar commercial sells soap. Twenty-five minutes worth of glorification of violence sell violence." Hence, having fed our children death and horror as entertainment, we should not be surprised by the outcome. But we are not powerless to address the problem. People need to respond to the problem of media violence in a responsible manner. If we take steps at both the national level-by dealing with the marketing of, and access to, violent media-and at the most local of levels-by empowering parents to exercise greater control over the material their children access-we can significantly reduce the impact of violent media on the young people. With respect to national reform, the Senate recently adopted the "Violent and Repeat Juvenile Offender Accountability and Rehabilitation Act of 1999" (the "Juvenile Justice Act"). This legislation, summarized below, adopts a comprehensive approach which confronts youth violence on several fronts, including media violence.

Self-regulatory Programs

On June 1, 1999, the then US President Clinton asked the Federal Trade Commission and the Department of Justice to undertake a study of whether the movie, music recording, and computer and video game industries market and advertise products with violent content to youngsters. The President's request paralleled Congressional calls for such a study. The President raised two specific questions: Do the industries promote products they themselves acknowledge warrant parental caution in venues where children make up a substantial percentage of the audience? And are these advertisements intended to attract children and teenagers? For all three segments of the entertainment industry, the answers are plainly "yes."

Although the motion picture, music recording and electronic game industries have taken steps to identify content that may not be appropriate for children, companies in those industries routinely target children under 17 as the audience for movies, music and games that their own rating or labeling systems say are inappropriate for children or warrant parental caution due to their violent content. Moreover, children under 17 frequently are able to buy tickets to R-rated movies without being accompanied by an adult and can easily purchase music recordings and electronic games that have a parental advisory label or are restricted to an older audience.

The practice of pervasive and aggressive marketing of violent movies, music and electronic games to children undermines the credibility of the industries' ratings and labels. Such marketing also frustrates parents' attempts to make informed decisions about their children's exposure to violent content.

For years parents, social scientists, criminologists, educators, policymakers, health care providers, journalists and others have struggled to understand how and why some children turn to violence. They generally have agreed that exposure to violence in entertainment media alone does not cause a child to commit a violent act and that it is not the sole, or even necessarily the most important, factor contributing to youth aggression, anti-social attitudes and violence. Nonetheless, there is widespread agreement that it is a cause for concern.

The Commission reported that a majority of the investigations into the impact of media violence on children find that there is a high correlation between exposure to media violence and aggressive, and at times violent, behavior. In addition, a number of research efforts report that exposure to media violence is correlated with increased acceptance of violent behavior in others, as well as an exaggerated perception of the amount of violence in society.

For their part, the entertainment industries have recognized these concerns and taken steps to alert parents to violent or explicit content through self-regulatory product rating or labeling programs. Self-regulation by these industries is especially important considering the First Amendment protections that prohibit government regulation of content in most instances.

The self-regulatory programs of the motion picture, music recording and electronic game industries each address violence, as well as sexual content, language, drug use and other explicit content that may be of concern to parents. In keeping with the President's request, the Commission focused on the marketing of entertainment products designated as violent under these systems. In its analysis, the Commission accepted each industry's determination of whether a particular motion picture, music recording or electronic game contains violent content; the Commission did not examine the content itself.

The motion picture industry uses a rating board to rate virtually all movies released in the United States, requires the age-related rating to appear in advertising and makes some effort to review ads for rated movies to ensure that their content is suitable for general audiences.

The music recording industry recommends the use of a general parental advisory label on music with "explicit content." The decision to place a parental advisory label on a recording is made by the artist and the music publishing company and involves no independent third-party review; nor does the industry provide for any review of marketing and advertising.

In late August 2000, the recording industry trade association recommended that recording companies not advertise explicit-content labeled recordings in media outlets with a majority under-17 audience. The electronic game industry requires games to be labeled with age- and content-based rating information and requires that the rating information appear in advertising. Only the electronic game industry has adopted a rule prohibiting its marketers from targeting advertising for games to children below the age designations indicated by the rating.

The Commission carefully examined the structure of these rating and labeling systems, and studied how these self-regulatory systems work in practice. The Commission found that despite the variations in the three industries' systems, the outcome is consistent: individual companies in each industry routinely market to children the very products that have the industries' own parental warnings or ratings with age restrictions due to their violent content. Indeed, for many of these products, the Commission found evidence of marketing and media plans that expressly target children under 17.

In addition, the companies' marketing and media plans showed strategies to promote and advertise their products in the media outlets most likely to reach children under 17, including those television programs ranked as the "most popular" with the under-17 age group, such as Xena: Warrior Princess, South Park and Buffy the Vampire Slayer; magazines and Internet sites with a majority or substantial under-17 audience, such as Game Pro, Seventeen and Right On!, as well as mtv.com, ubl.com and happypuppy.com; and teen hangouts, such as game rooms, pizza parlors and sporting apparel stores.

Movies: Of the 44 movies rated R for violence the Commission selected for its study, the Commission found that 35, or 80 percent, were targeted to children under 17. Marketing plans for 28 of those 44, or 64 percent, contained express statements that the film's target audience included children under 17. For example, one plan for a violent R-rated film stated, "Our goal was to find the elusive teen target audience and make sure everyone between the ages of 12-18 was exposed to the film."

Though the marketing plans for the remaining seven R-rated films did not expressly identify an under-17 target audience, they led the Commission to conclude that children under 17 were targeted nonetheless. That is, the plans were either extremely similar to the plans of the films that did identify an under-17 target audience, or they detailed actions synonymous with targeting that age group, such as promoting the film in high schools or in publications with majority under-17 audiences.

Music: Of the 55 music recordings with explicit content labels the Commission selected for its study, marketing plans for 15, or 27 percent, expressly identified teenagers as part of their target audience. One such plan, for instance, stated that its "Target audience" was "Alternative/urban, rock, pop, hardcore - 12-34."

The marketing documents for the remaining 40 explicit-content labeled recordings examined did not expressly state the age of the target audience, but they detailed the same methods of marketing as the plans that specifically identified teens as part of their target audience, including placing advertising in media that would reach a majority or substantial percentage of children under 17.

Games. Of the 118 electronic games with a Mature rating for violence the Commission selected for its study, 83, or 70 percent, targeted children under 17. The marketing plans for 60 of these, or 51 percent, expressly included children under 17 in their target audience. For example, one plan for a game rated Mature for its violent content described its "target audience" as "Males 12-17 - Primary Males 18-34 - Secondary." Another plan referred to the target market as "Males 17-34 due to M rating (the true target is males 12-34)."

Documents for the remaining 23 games showed plans to advertise in magazines or on television shows with a majority or substantial under-17 audience. Most of the plans that targeted an under-17 audience set age 12 as the younger end of the spectrum, but a few plans for violent Mature-rated games targeted children as young as six.

Further, most retailers make little effort to restrict children's access to products with violent content. Surveys conducted for the Commission in May through July 2000 found that just over half the movie theaters admitted children ages 13 to 16 to R-rated films even when not accompanied by an adult. The Commission's surveys also indicate that unaccompanied children have various strategies to see R-rated movies when theaters refuse to sell them tickets. Additionally, the Commission's surveys showed that unaccompanied children ages 13 to 16 were able to buy both explicit content recordings and Mature-rated electronic games 85 percent of the time.

Although consumer surveys show that parents value the existing rating and labeling systems, they also show that parents' use and understanding of the systems vary. The surveys also consistently reveal high levels of parental concern about violence in the movies, music and video games their children see, listen to and play. These concerns can only be heightened by the extraordinary degree to which young people today are immersed in entertainment media, as well as by recent technological advances such as realistic and interactive video games. The survey responses indicate that parents want and welcome help in identifying which entertainment products might not be suitable for their children.

The Commission believes that all three industries should take additional action to enhance their self-regulatory efforts. The industries should:

1. *Establish or expand codes that prohibit target marketing to children and impose sanctions for violations.* All three industries should improve the usefulness of their ratings and labels by establishing codes that prohibit marketing R-rated/M-rated/explicit-labeled products in media or venues with a substantial under-17 audience. In addition, the Commission suggests that each industry's trade associations monitor and encourage their members' compliance with these policies and impose meaningful sanctions for non-compliance.

2. *Increase compliance at the retail level.* Restricting children's retail access to entertainment containing violent content is an essential complement to

restricting the placement of advertising. This can be done by checking identification or requiring parental permission before selling tickets to R movies, and by not selling or renting products labeled "Explicit" or rated R or M, to children.

3. *Increase parental understanding of the ratings and labels.* For parents to make informed choices about their children's entertainment, they must understand the ratings and the labels, as well as the reasons for them. That means the industries should all include the reasons for the rating or the label in advertising and product packaging and continue their efforts to educate parents - and children - about the meanings of the ratings and descriptors. Industry should also take steps to better educate parents about the ratings and labels.

The Commission believes the industries can do a better job of helping parents choose appropriate entertainment for their children by providing clear and conspicuous notification of violent content. Industry selfregulation also should support parents' decisions by prohibiting the direct sale and marketing to children of products labeled as inappropriate or warranting parental guidance due to their violent content.

Implementation of the specific suggestions outlined above would significantly improve the present self-regulatory regimes. However, that mere publication of codes is not sufficient. Self-regulatory programs can work only if the concerned industry associations actively monitor compliance and ensure that violations have consequences.

Motion Picture Industry Self-regulatory System

The motion picture rating system, which was established in 1968 as a joint venture between the Motion Picture Association of America ("MPAA") and the National Association of Theatre Owners ("NATO"), is the longest-running of the self-regulatory systems the Commission examined. It was crafted following a pair of U.S. Supreme Court decisions upholding the power of states to regulate children's access to materials protected by the First Amendment.To curtail a proliferation of local censorship boards, the major film studios and theaters created a single, nationwide rating system.

Although the system is voluntary, all MPAA member companies have agreed not to distribute a film without a rating.As a result, the vast majority of films are rated. A high percentage of parents are familiar with motion picture ratings (surveys show more than 90% awareness) and a large majority (more than 70%) find the ratings useful.

In examining the motion picture industry's self-regulatory program and the marketing of films to children, the Commission reviewed documents provided by the MPAA and its member studios; NATO and its member theaters, as well as theater chains that do not belong to NATO; and publicly available materials concerning the system.

More specifically, the Commission studied the marketing of 44 violent R-rated films and 20 violent PG-13-rated films distributed by nine major studios from 1995-1999.In selecting these films, the Commission chose R- and PG-13-rated movies that the MPAA's rating body had determined should receive such a rating at least in part for violence, including films the industry trade press had referred to as teen or children's movies. Thus, these 64 films are not a random sample of all violent R and PG-13 movies produced by the MPAA member studios over the relevant time period.

The Commission studied "media plans," which outline where the television, radio, print, and Internet advertising was placed and describe the target audiences the studios intended the advertising to reach; promotional reports for many of these films, which detail the vast array of promotional activities used to generate consumer awareness and interest in a movie; and studio research conducted on test audiences for the films and their advertising. The studios and the theater chains also supplied trailer reports detailing which trailers preceded certain features.

The motion picture industry has put in place a formalized rating system that is designed to impose a measure of objectivity and consistency across the broad array of subjects and styles encompassed by modern filmmaking. Although this system has been criticized over the years,it has remained intact for more than 30 years and is wellestablished with the American public.

The current categories for film ratings, as defined by the MPAA and NATO, follow:

— *G : General Audiences - All ages admitted:* Signifies that the film rated contains nothing most parents will consider offensive for even their youngest children to see or hear. Nudity, sex scenes, and scenes of drug use are absent; violence is minimal; snippets of dialogue may go beyond polite conversation but do not go beyond common everyday expressions.

— ***PG** : Parental Guidance Suggested - Some material may not be suitable for children.* Signifies that the film rated may contain some material parents might not like to expose to their young children – material that will clearly need to be examined or inquired about before children are allowed to attend the film. Explicit sex scenes and scenes of drug use are absent; nudity, if present, is seen only briefly, horror and violence do not exceed moderate levels.

— ***PG-13** : Parents Strongly Cautioned - Some material may be inappropriate for children under 13.* Signifies that the film rated may be inappropriate for pre-teens. Parents should be especially careful about letting their younger children attend. Rough or persistent violence is absent; sexually-oriented nudity is generally absent; some scenes of drug use may be seen; some use of one of the harsher sexually-derived words may be heard.

— ***R** : Restricted - Under 17 requires accompanying parent or adult guardian (age varies in some jurisdictions).* Signifies that the rating board has concluded that the film rated may contain some adult material. Parents are urged to learn more about the film before taking their children to see it. An R may be assigned due to, among other things, a film's use of language, theme, violence, sex or its portrayal of drug use.

— ***NC-17:** No one 17 and Under Admitted.* Signifies that the rating board believes that most American parents would feel that the film is patently adult and that children age 17 and under should not be admitted to it. The film may contain explicit sex scenes, an accumulation of sexually-oriented language, and/or scenes of excessive violence. The NC-17 designation does not, however, signify that the rated film is obscene or pornographic in terms of sex, language or violence.

Each film assigned a rating other than G also receives a brief explanation for the film's rating, *e.g.*, "Rated R for terror, violence and language," or "Rated PG-13 for intense sci-fi violence, some sexuality and brief nudity."

The Classification and Ratings Administration ("CARA") determines the ratings and explanations. Qualifications for membership in CARA are parenting experience and no connection to the film industry. Currently, CARA has 12 members (known as raters), and two Co-Chairs, all of whom are approved by, and serve at the discretion of, the President of the MPAA.

A Policy Review Committee consisting of MPAA and NATO officials sets the rules that govern CARA procedures. This Committee instructs CARA board members to give each film the rating that, based on theme, language, nudity and sexual content, violence, drug use, and "other relevant matters,"they think most American parents would consider appropriate for viewing by children.A simple majority vote determines the rating.

The studio submitting the film can accept the CARA rating, appeal, or edit the film to achieve a less severe rating. Rating appeals are rare;more often, a distributor will edit the film to achieve a desired rating. However, if a studio chooses to appeal the rating, an Appeals Board views the film. Unlike the original CARA raters, who have no connection to the film industry, the Appeals Board is made up of industry members, with MPAA and NATO members comprising the vast majority of the votes.For an appeal to be successful, two thirds of the Appeals Board must conclude that the rating assigned by CARA was "clearly erroneous."

Violence is one of the factors that CARA members specifically consider in assigning ratings to the films they review. According to the MPAA, PG-13 films have no rough or persistent violence, and the existence of such violence will cause a film to be rated R.Nevertheless, the Commission's study of the ratings explanations indicates that CARA often describes the violence in PG-13 films in terms synonymous with rough and persistent violence, for example, as "intense," "strong," "disturbing," "brutal," "graphic," "shocking," "non-stop,' and "pervasive." These words are identical or similar to words often used to describe violence in R-rated movies,causing some to question the usefulness of the ratings for helping parents distinguish the amount and kind of violence in PG-13 films from that in R-rated films.Parental uncertainty over the violent content contained in PG-13 films is of concern because these films frequently are marketed to children as young as six.

Advertising for Content and Rating Information

The motion picture industry's self-regulatory system is the only one of the three examined by the Commission that includes substantive review and pre-approval of advertising. For a film to use the MPAA-trademarked rating, all advertising materials for a film, including all television and radio commercials, print advertising, Web sites, and trailers, must be approved by the MPAA's Advertising Administration. The Advertising Administration does not approve advertising for products related to motion pictures, such as action figures, toys, clothing, or other licensed products.

Review by the Advertising Administration is designed to accomplish two goals. The first is to ensure the accurate dissemination of the rating symbol in all advertising for a film. MPAA rules require that a film's letter rating be displayed in all advertising. The Commission's review suggests that the Advertising Administration generally achieves this goal.

The Advertising Administration's other goal is to ensure that the content of a film's advertising, regardless of the film's rating, is appropriate for even the youngest audience. The MPAA requires the Advertising Administration to disapprove advertising if it would not pass muster with most parents as suitable for young children; that is, the content of the advertising must be the equivalent of a G-rated movie.A film distributor that disagrees with the Advertising Administration's decision regarding the content of an advertisement can appeal the decision directly to the MPAA President.

The Commission's review indicates that the Advertising Administration is less successful at meeting its second goal. Theatrical trailers illustrate the point. The Advertising Administration approves two types of trailers, which, based on the Commission's review of studio media plans, appear to be the first widely disseminated advertisements for a film. The first type, known as an "all audience" trailer, is for general audiences and can be shown before any feature film. According to the MPAA, "There will be, in 'all audiences' trailers, no scenes that caused the feature to be rated PG, PG-13, R, or NC-17."The second type of trailer is for restricted audiences and can be shown only before films rated R or NC-17.A review of materials submitted to the Commission suggests that, although the

Advertising Administration restricts the material allowed in all audience trailers, it does not require the studios to remove everything that would cause a movie to be given a rating more restrictive than G. Trailers are approved by the Advertising Administration and shown in theaters long before a film is rated; consequently, for these "teaser trailers,"the Advertising Administration has no way to know what will cause the raters to rate a film PG or higher.And CARA raters do not evaluate trailers or other advertising.

The Commission found numerous examples when trailers approved for "all audiences" contained material that the Advertising Administration's Handbook says might "engender criticism by parents."For example, the "all audience" trailer for *I Know What You Did Last Summer* contained verbal references to mutilations (references to decapitation and to a person being "gutted with a hook") and drug use. A trailer for *Scream* 2 contained a verbal reference to mutilation (that a woman had been stabbed seven times) and several visual depictions of violence against women (women being pursued by a masked, knife-wielding killer).Television advertising also is affected when material causing a rating more restrictive than G is not edited out of an "all audience" trailer.

Television commercials for movies generally are shortened versions of the trailers; they thus may contain some of the same violent material. Although the MPAA states that "TV spots containing sexual references, violence, blood or profanity are not acceptable,"the Commission's review shows that the television networks sometimes require the deletion of certain scenes or restrict the airing of commercials the MPAA had approved for general audiences because the advertisement is too violent.

Motion Picture Marketing

A central question the Commission was asked to address in the study is whether violent entertainment products are being marketed to children. With respect to the film industry, the answer is plainly "yes." The Commission's review indicates that motion picture studios routinely advertise movies rated R for violence to children under 17 and movies rated PG-13 for violence to children under 13. The marketing of a motion picture begins long before the film is rated.The studios exhibit rough cuts of the actual film as well as its core advertisements (trailers, TV commercials, and print ads) to test audiences, and conduct detailed research on many aspects of the film. Movie marketers choose audiences for these tests to meet defined demographics, including age parameters set by the studios. They conduct advertising research to measure the interestgenerating potential of the advertisement, identify the moviegoers most attracted by the advertisements, and determine the messages conveyed.

Media advertising for a film also begins before the film is rated, or even completed. Six months to a year before a film opens, teaser trailers appear in theaters and on the Internet. Television commercials for summer releases may air during the Super Bowl in January.

Newspaper and magazine advertising and outdoor banners also appear months before opening.Two to four weeks before a film opens, studios may launch a massive media blitz designed to saturate the marketplace. Because studio research suggests that most moviegoers learn about new films through television advertising, it is the most important aspect of many motion picture advertising campaigns. The studios also use radio, print, outdoor advertising, the Internet, and promotional activities to generate interest in a film. During a campaign, studios receive industrywide tracking reports - up to three times per week - measuring the campaign's success among various age groups, including children aged 12-17.

The motion picture industry's self-regulatory system does not restrict the placement of advertising materials for R and PG-13 films because the MPAA takes the view that children are appropriate targets for such films, so long as parental accompaniment or guidance is provided. The marketing documents reviewed by the Commission indicate extensive marketing - and, in many instances, explicit targeting - of violent R films to children under the age of 17 and of violent PG-13 films to children under 13.

Specifically, the documents show that 35 of the 44 R-rated films studied by the Commission, or 80%, were targeted to children under 17.[76] Media plans or promotional reports for 28 of those 44 films, or 64%, contain express statements that the film's target audience included children under 17. Marketing materials for seven other R-rated films also appeared to be targeting those under 17, though they did not expressly identify a target audience under 17. The plans for these seven films were either strikingly similar to the plans that did expressly target those under 17, or they detailed actions synonymous with targeting that age group.

Studio records also indicate that youngsters under the age of 17 were included in some marketing research activities. Thirty-three of the 44 R-rated films tested either a rough cut of the film or the film's advertising on an audience that included teens under 17. Although most of this research was conducted on those 15 and older, research for eight R-rated films included 12- year-olds, and research for at least one other R-rated film was conducted on children as young as 10.

Promoting violent PG-13-rated films to those under 13, while not as pervasive, is not unusual. Marketing materials for 20 films rated PG-13 for violence revealed that nine, or 45%, targeted children 11 and younger.

Television Advertising

R-rated films: Studio research shows that most moviegoers, and teens in particular, become aware of movies through television. Accordingly, studio media plans detail massive television campaigns. Of the 35 R-rated movies that targeted children under 17, studio media plans indicate that 26 designed at least part of their television campaign around a target audience including people aged 12 and above.

The studios repeatedly advertised films rated R for violence on television programs that were the highest rated among teens or where teens comprised the largest percentage of the audience. The plans sometimes referred to these programs as "teen-oriented." When studios targeted films to a particularly young audience, they increased significantly the frequency of advertising on those shows and excluded other programming. To reach teenage audiences more effectively, studios target advertising for certain times of day. Studio marketing materials indicate that the best way to reach younger viewers is to purchase advertising on local stations - a process referred to as "Spot TV buys" - on weekends, and during the "early fringe" and "prime access" hours, i.e., after school and before prime-time network programming begins at 8 p.m. The studios advertised violent R-rated movies to children under 17 with cable television campaigns that were remarkably similar to each other.

MTV, with its core demographic of 12-24,87 was the largest advertising cable outlet for almost every motion picture the Commission examined, in terms of both the quantity of ads and the target audience reached. Indeed, the younger the target audience, the more the studios tended to advertise on MTV. For some of the movies targeting particularly young audiences, it was not uncommon for a studio to use MTV to achieve over 50% of its cable audience exposure.

PG-13-rated films: Seven of the nine PG-13-rated films that were targeted to children 11 and younger were advertised on afternoon and Saturday morning cartoon programs. Marketing plans also included advertising on the Cartoon Network and Nickelodeon.

An analysis of the television campaigns for PG-13 films targeting youngsters 6-11 indicates that many of the television programs popular with teens and used heavily to promote R-rated movies, also are very popular with children 6-11. As one marketing plan for a PG-13 movie targeting those 6-11 stated, "Other programs, such as Buffy The Vampire Slayer, WWF and WCW Wrestling cross over to Children 6-11 and local television buys targeted this group as well." This plan also showed that Xena: Warrior Princess - used in advertising for virtually every R-rated movie the Commission examined - was as popular with children 6-11 as it was with males 12-17. MTV is also popular with children 6-11. Thus, although the Commission found little indication that R-rated films were deliberately being marketed to children under 12, those young children nevertheless had substantial exposure to the television advertising for R-rated films as well.

Trailers

Trailers are a unique form of advertising. Trailer placement is governed by unwritten agreements between the studios and theaters through their principal trade associations. Studios do not pay the theaters to show their trailers. Completed features are sent to theaters with one trailer physically attached; other unattached trailers are sent to the theaters with a request that they be shown with a particular feature. The MPAA and NATO have agreed to limit trailer length and to require only that theaters play the attached trailer. Although unattached trailers are played at the discretion of the theater, the studios exert pressure on the theaters to adhere to their requests. Studios hire "trailer checkers" to verify that theaters are showing their trailers, and theaters may be concerned that if they do not show the requested trailers, a studio might not book a future hit feature with them.

In general, theaters do not show trailers for R- and PG-13-rated movies before children's animated features.

In 1989, NATO passed a resolution stating: "All trailers shown with a 'G' rated film should be compatible therewith, and theatre owners should be especially sensitive to this situation to the end that the theatre going public will be entirely comfortable taking young children to view 'G' rated motion pictures." NATO adopted this resolution due to complaints received from irate parents over the strong content of "all audience" trailers shown at films geared to young audiences. For this reason, the major theater chains have adopted policies to limit trailer placement to within one rating of the feature presentation. The net effect of this trailer placement policy, however, is that previews for R-rated films are shown to audiences containing substantial numbers of youngsters under 17:

trailer requests reviewed by the Commission show that the studios routinely seek to place trailers (both attached and unattached) for R-rated movies at PG-13-rated features, including those PG-13 features the Commission determined were marketed to children 11 and younger. In addition, the theaters appear to grant exceptions to the "within one rating" policy.

For example, trailer check reports reviewed by the Commission show that Star Wars Episode 1: The Phantom Menace, rated PG, was regularly preceded by trailers for such films as The General's Daughter ("Rated R for graphic images relating to sexual violence including a strong rape scene, some perverse sexuality, nudity and language"), South Park ("Rated R for pervasive vulgar language and crude sexual humor, and for some violent images"), and The Beach ("Rated R for violence, some strong sexuality, language and drug content").

Promotional and Street Marketing

The studios use a wide array of promotional activities to generate interest in a film. Although the majority of these activities are directed to a very broad audience, some are directed to children.

R-rated films: One of the most popular methods the studios used to attract teens to R-rated films was to distribute free passes to movie screenings and free merchandise related to the film (such as t-shirts, tatoos, and mini-posters) at places where teens congregate. As one marketing plan for an R-rated film stated:

> [O]ur goal was to find the elusive teen target audience and make sure everyone between the ages of 12-18 was exposed to the film. To do so, we went beyond the media partners by enlisting young, hip

> "Teen Street Teams" to distribute items at strategic teen "hangouts" such as malls, teen clothing stores, sporting events, Driver's Ed classes, arcades and numerous other locations.

Although only one studio described this promotional device in such direct terms, all the studios that provided details of their promotional activities used this tactic to attract teens.

PG-13-rated films: Toys, children's clothing, and fast food appear to be the primary promotional methods for generating interest in PG-13 movies among children 11 and younger.

Three studios had licensing arrangements with toy and apparel companies for children's merchandise based on violent PG-13 films. Although these agreements are intended to generate their own revenue as well as to generate interest in seeing a film, the marketing materials reviewed by the Commission show they constitute an important facet of film promotion.

Radio and Print Advertising

Radio advertising, although used less extensively than television, was an integral part of many advertising campaigns.99 Marketing materials from five of the studios showed that radio was particularly useful in attracting audiences under 17. The studios also used print advertising to target R-rated movies to teens. Magazines with majority under-17 audiences, such as Teen, Jump, YM, DC Comics Teen, or Marvel Comics, contained advertisements for numerous R-rated films. In addition, six of the studios used print media distributed exclusively in schools - Planet Report and/or Fast Times - to advertise R-rated movies. Planet Report is published by a company that distributes posters and other promotional items to at least 8,000 schools, including high schools and elementary schools. Fast Times, a news and entertainment magazine, is used as a high school teaching aid and often is assigned as mandatory reading to high school students.

Internet Marketing

The motion picture studios also promote their films by establishing an "official" Web site for each movie they release. Web sites generally have trailers for the movie available for downloading and viewing, as well as background information on the film's cast and creators. The studios include the address for the official movie site in virtually all print advertising and also place banner ads on other sites that link directly to the official site. For the R-rated films that targeted teens, the studios placed banner ads on sites with high teen usage.

An important feature of the Internet is that it provides another outlet to show trailers for movies. Before widespread use of the Internet, trailers were limited to theaters. Now, trailers, in addition to being available on a movie's official site, also are available on numerous theater sites and through aggregator sites, many of which are independent from the studios and provide reviews and information about films.

The proliferation of trailers online presents some obvious problems: "restricted trailers," those with content the MPAA has determined not to be acceptable for "all audiences," can easily be accessed by children under 17; in addition, the strong content contained in some "all audience" trailers is also accessible on the Internet by those under 17. The Commission's review found restricted trailers for American Pie and Road Trip posted on official

Web sites that can be accessed as easily as "all audience" trailers by children under 17.

Box Office Enforcement

As partners in the industry's self-regulatory system, movie theaters have urged the motion picture studios to include explanations for ratings in print advertising, and they also play a central role in trailer placement. Nevertheless, enforcement of the R rating category - ensuring that patrons under 17, without parental involvement, do not see R-rated films at theaters - remains the fundamental role of the theater. In fulfilling this role, the theaters must strike a delicate balance between the need for enforcement and the need to maintain a friendly and welcoming environment.

Despite the official policy that children under 17 should not be admitted to an R-rated movie unless accompanied by a parent or guardian, such children gain access in a variety of ways. They may purchase a ticket for the film themselves; have a sibling, friend, or stranger over the age of 17 purchase it for them; or, in a multitheater complex, purchase a ticket to a PG-13- or lower-rated film and then, once past the ticket taker, go into the auditorium showing the R-rated picture. In a multiplex theater, meaningful enforcement of the age restrictions reflected in the MPAA ratings requires that attention be paid at two different places in the theater: the ticket window and the auditorium entrance.

Material from the eight largest domestic theater chains indicates that they have taken responsible measures to increase enforcement of the minimum age requirement for the purchase of tickets to R-rated features since the

Columbine shootings. In a June 1999 public announcement with President Clinton, NATO promised stricter enforcement of the MPAA guidelines. Specifically, NATO announced that all its member theaters should require, at the box office, photo identification of unaccompanied young patrons seeking admission to R-rated films.

Despite these enhanced efforts, an undercover shopper survey of 395 theaters conducted for the Commission in May through July 2000 found that just over half of the theaters enforced the age restrictions at the box office. Theaters refused to sell tickets to R-rated movies to unaccompanied 13- to 16-year-old children 54% of the time; youngsters successfully purchased those tickets 46% of the time. The same percentage of theaters that did not admit unaccompanied children (54%) also posted information about the rating system or theater enforcement policy.

NATO has suggested several ways theater chains might expand enforcement beyond box office identification checks: posting ushers to check for proof of age at the doors of features expected to attract a high proportion of teens; stamping the hands of patrons who have shown proof of age to the cashier, so they later can be checked for proof of age more easily; and, in multiplexes, when and where possible, showing similarly rated features in the same area of the complex.

The Commission's review indicates that, to date, the major theater chains have adopted very few of these suggestions. Four of the eight chains may require further proof of age by either the ticket taker or an usher posted at the auditorium entrance. The rest rely solely on the cashier. None of the theaters appears to have implemented NATO's other suggestions.

Retailing of Movie Videos

Children's access to violent movies on home video differs according to whether the video is rented or purchased. Parents have significant controls over the videos their children rent because of limitations established by the major rental outlets. To be eligible for rental privileges, a customer of a video rental store usually must be 18 and have a credit card, making it difficult for children to rent videos independent of their parents' membership.

Blockbuster Video and Hollywood Video, the dominant home video membership stores, have responded to parental concerns by adopting policies that give parents the option to restrict the videos rented by their children. Under Blockbuster Video's policy, parents must affirmatively give their consent to their children's rental of R-rated movies.

Hollywood Video's policy is the opposite: parental consent to rent R-rated videos is presumed and parents must opt to place restrictions on the account. Another large retail chain follows a discretionary policy: it gives individual stores autonomy in deciding whether to permit the rental of R-rated movies to minors. Although renting R-rated videos usually requires a degree of parental involvement, the direct purchase of such videos often does not.

Home videos are sold at a wide variety of locations, ranging from specialized video stores and small convenience stores to large discount merchants, supermarkets, and the Internet. The Commission reviewed the policies of eight major retailers that sell home videos at traditional "bricks and mortar" stores. Only three of these informed the Commission that they have policies restricting the sale of R-rated videos to children under 17. These three retailers also rent videos, and thus may be more attuned to the issue of parental consent in this area.

All of the online retailers contacted by the Commission provide MPAA ratings information. However, these same retailers generally do not have express policies restricting the online sale of R-rated videos to children. One retailer stated that it relies on the purchaser's use of a credit card as a proxy for parental approval. The other retailers did not indicate whether they do so as well.

Parental Advisory Program of Recording Industry

The Recording Industry Association of America ("RIAA") created a parental advisory program in 1985 in response to concerns of parent groups about children's exposure to music with mature themes. Under the program, music recordings that contain explicit lyrics, including strong language or graphic references to violence, sex, or drug use, are identified with a parental advisory label.

The RIAA describes the parental advisory label as a tool for record companies to use to alert parents to explicit lyrics. The decision to label a recording is made by individual record companies and their artists. RIAA members, as well as non-member companies, use the advisory.

In examining the music recording industry's parental advisory labeling program, the Commission reviewed documents provided by the RIAA and the National Association of Recording Merchandisers ("NARM"), as well as publicly available materials. In addition, because each recording company labels its own explicit-content recordings, the Commission analyzed documents provided by the major recording companies - BMG Entertainment, EMI Recorded Music, North America, Sony Music Entertainment, Inc., Warner Music Group, Inc., and UMG Recordings, Inc. (Universal) - and their affiliated record companies (together "the recording companies") that explain their individual procedures for determining which recordings need to display the parental advisory label.

In addition, the Commission studied the marketing plans, advertisements, and advertisement dissemination schedules for 55 full-length recordings with the parental advisory label, all of which were top sellers in 1999. Because the recording companies could not specify which recordings received the parental advisory label due to violent content, as opposed to some other explicit content, these companies produced materials for top-selling recordings labeled for any reason due to their "explicit" content (which could include strong language and/or depictions of sex, violence, or substance use).Also, because the RIAA's label makes no recommendations to parents about the age appropriateness of recordings with explicit lyrics, the Commission applied the age limit (17) of the movie and electronic game industry self-regulatory programs to its analysis of whether the recording industry is marketing explicit-content labeled recordings to children.

Unlike the film and electronic game self-regulatory systems, the recording industry labeling program does not have a rating board to determine which music recordings should display the parental advisory label. Nor does the RIAA provide standardized procedures or other guidance as to when a recording should display a parental advisory. Instead, the decision is made by each company for its own products. The parental advisory label is black and white, measures 1" x 5/8" and says "Parental Advisory, Explicit Content."

According to the RIAA, with about 60,000 recordings released each year, the artists and recording companies themselves can make the labeling decision most efficiently. In addition, the RIAA believes that because the parental advisory label is meant to flag for parents any potentially offensive material, it makes sense for a "sensitive and sophisticated" labeler at each company to make the labeling decision. Therefore, to report on the labeling process, the Commission reviewed the practices of the five major recording companies.

According to the recording companies, the decision to label is subjective, and often made on a case-by-case basis. None of the companies has adopted written policies or guidelines defining "explicit" content in music and none memorializes why a particular recording received the advisory. One company reported that its employees, often in partnership with the artists involved, make "good faith judgments about what kinds of lyrics and depictions parents might find offensive, because of racial epithets, vulgarities, curse words, sexual references, violence, and drug descriptions."

Another company evaluates the content of every recording on the basis of various factors, including, but not limited to: explicit exhortations of sex, violence, illicit drug use, or suicide; exhortations of violence against any specific named real person or peace officer; offensive language generally and use of objectionable words; overall impression, including generally nihilistic world view, pervasive misogyny or racial/minority stereotyping. "The ultimate judgment call of whether the content of a recording warrants the [parental advisory label] is made in light of the message and identity of the artist, the current social climate, and, perhaps most importantly, straightforward common sense," the company said.

Documents from the three remaining companies suggest that they evaluate the content of a recording based on a cursory review of the lyrics. According to these companies, they may decide to label a recording as soon as they hear a number of expletives on one song, without listening to an album's entire content. One company explained that because the RIAA system involves a single label, a more thorough analysis is unnecessary, and that "the process is not distinctly tailored to differentiate among 'violent content,' sex, language, or any other reason as the basis for stickering." If a company and/or an artist determines that a recording contains explicit content, the RIAA recommends using the label on the packaging of all cassettes, CDs, vinyl records, and music videotapes. According to the RIAA, the label should measure 1" x 5/8" and should be part of the permanent packaging under the cellophane shrink wrap, rather than a peel-off sticker.

The Commission's review of the packaging of 55 top-selling CDs that bore the parental advisory label indicates that the recording companies do not uniformly follow the RIAA's suggestions for using the label. In one company's case, 91% of the CD labels met the RIAA labeling parameters; in another company's case, none of the CDs - 0% - was labeled according to RIAA suggestions. The Commission noted the following:

— The advisory labels on 27 of the recordings (50%) met the RIAA recommendations for size, placement, and format.

— The labels on 41 of the recordings (75%) were incorporated directly into the CD packaging; the labels on the remaining 14 CDs (25%) were removable stickers attached to the CD case.

— A total of 10 of the removable stickers provided other information about popular songs on the CD in and around the advisory, tending to obscure the message on the advisory.

— Twenty-two of the advisories (39%) were smaller than the RIAA's recommended size.

In addition, a later review of the labels on 25 current top-selling labeled recordings also showed that the advisory often is smaller than the RIAA specifies or is a peel-off sticker. Although not specifically recommended by the RIAA, the recording companies routinely create and sell edited or "clean" versions of the explicit-content labeled recordings. According to one recording company, an edited version "provides listeners with the option of purchasing an artist's work without the explicit content as identified by [the recording company and] . . . provides an alternative to retailers and other media outlets that opt not to sell, disseminate or promote the unedited versions of the stickered recordings." Explicit or unedited versions of recordings usually outsell the edited version, often by over 10 times. In creating an edited version, one company states that it:

> often works closely with the artists to determine the necessary changes. In some recordings any explicit content is simply taken out, while in other instances new lyrics or sounds are added to replace those in the stickered version. These changes are made on a case by case basis with the focus centered on the deletion of any explicit content while making minimal changes to the artistic expression.

The company further acknowledges that "there remain in the edited versions of the CDs identified . . . instances of language, situations, and phrases that reasonably might be considered 'violent' without distorting standard English usage." Its justification for leaving such lyrics in the edited version is "there is also in popular children's fare (cowboy adventures, military exploits, fairy tales, cartoons, etc.) a great deal that is similarly 'violent,' but for which no one would advocate special labeling or warning." Creating an edited version is not always feasible, however. According to one company, if the controversial content is essential to the artist's message, the recording company may not release an edited version. The decision to create an edited version, this company said, also "may turn on the practical consequences of editing. . . .[A]n edited version may not be produced if the editing process would eliminate the preponderance of the lyrics."

Although the lyrics on the two versions may vary, the CD packaging often does not, except that the explicit version bears the parental advisory label. When the CD packaging itself contains "explicit content," the artwork used for the explicit and edited versions may differ. Similarly, when the packaging for both versions lists the songs, the edited versions often replace any profanity in song titles with asterisks.

Access to important information about explicit recordings The parental advisory label covers a wide range of content, including violence, sex, and/or drug use, without regard to the fact that some parents may be more concerned with certain types of explicit content than with others. Although the RIAA agrees that parents need information about recordings to be able to make intelligent listening choices for their children, groups such as the American Academy of Pediatrics and the National Parent Teacher Association have expressed concern that the industry's "one-size-fits-all" approach does not provide enough information to parents. Unlike the motion picture and electronic game rating systems, the label does not provide reasons for the advisory label or "content descriptors" indicating the nature or the amount of the explicit content (e.g., strong language or graphic references to violence, sex, or drug use). Instead, one advisory covers a broad spectrum of content, including violence and/or sex.

Nor does the label specify the age groups for which an explicit-content labeled recording may be inappropriate; parents of a 7-year-old are given the same advisory as parents of a 12-year-old or a 16-year-old. Further, the industry does not provide a means for parents to obtain the lyrics of explicit-content labeled recordings. In fact, the Commission found that out of the 55 labeled CDs that it reviewed, only eight included lyrics for the songs in the packaging. Parental review of a recording may be hindered because the lyrics on many explicit songs are difficult to understand without repeated listening.

Focus groups conducted for the RIAA indicate that parents want a "visible and credible voluntary labeling program that helps them monitor the music their children purchase."

Consumer survey evidence suggests that the current labeling program may not provide parents with enough information about violent lyrics to help them make decisions about their children's listening choices. In a survey conducted for the Commission in May and June 2000, fewer than half of the parents (44%) surveyed viewed the parental advisory as "excellent" (12%) or "good" (32%) at informing them about the level of violence in music. And although 74% of parents surveyed reported being "very satisfied" or "somewhat satisfied" with the parental advisory label, only 9% of parents who restrict their children's music mentioned the advisory label when asked how they decide what music their children can listen to. Of the overall sample of parents, 45% use the advisory program at least some of the time.

According to a June 1999 Gallup poll, 74% of the respondents thought that music producers do not provide enough information about the violent content in lyrics of popular music for adults to make decisions about what is appropriate for children; 22% thought that the information was enough. The same poll found that 73% of parents believed that the music industry should place restrictions on the sale of recordings with violent content to children under 18, as well as provide information to the public about the violent content of recordings.

The current labeling program encourages an advisory on explicit music sold in CD, cassette, or album formats, but not on explicit music that is downloaded electronically and stored as a computer file (e.g., an MP3 file). Internet technology is making music available to a broad audience, and studies show that listening to and obtaining music in a digital format is increasingly popular with teenagers. The recording companies have begun to address the growing availability of digital music and to create their own systems of digital music distribution. However, no parental advisory labeling program exists for digital music.

Advertising Disclosure and Placement Standards

The RIAA has stated that the explicit content label is a tool designed "to provide a clear notice to parents to allow them to decide . . . what may or may not be appropriate music for their children." The RIAA program's single element has been a point-of-purchase disclosure on the packaging of a CD, cassette, or album. The labeling program has not addressed the advertising of explicit recordings, either in terms of whether the advisory label should appear in advertising or whether the recording companies should limit where they place ads for labeled recordings. The Commission's review of the music advertising submitted by the recording companies and by eight major music retailers shows that, while some ads for explicit recordings display the advisory, many do not. Moreover, when the label appears in advertising, it often is a black and white blur that is too small for consumers to read, or is obscured by pricing information.

A separate review of recent issues of magazines popular with teens shows that advertisements for explicit-content labeled recordings rarely display the parental advisory: only 18 (8%) of 234 print ads for labeled recordings displayed the advisory. Similarly, a review of artist, recording company, and music retailer Web sites shows that many of the online promotions for explicit recordings omit the parental advisory.

There are a few notable exceptions, however. Some recording company and retailer Web sites tell consumers about the explicit content of the recordings they are selling through text disclosures near the promotions. For example, Cash Money Records uses clear text disclosures -"Explicit Version" and "Clean Version" - directly below pictures of the individual recordings. Similarly, Amazon.com regularly includes the warning "EXPLICIT LYRICS" on its Web pages and in its print advertising. This advisory text is often presented in a large, easy-to-read notice. CDNow.com and TWEC.com also place the term "explicit" next to promotions for labeled albums and the term "edited" next to promotions for edited albums. However, because most advertisements for labeled recordings do not show the advisory label, parents may not have the notice they need to decide what music is appropriate for their children to purchase.

Most teens and many pre-teens make music purchase decisions without consulting their parents; therefore, advertisements may be parents' only advance source of information regarding the music their children are purchasing. Finally, it appears that the utility of the advisory label as an effective notice to parents has been diminished by the industry's lack of guidance on the marketing of explicit-content labeled music recordings to children.

In late August 2000, the RIAA recommended revisions to the parental advisory label program, to be effective October 1, 2000. According to the recommendation, the RIAA now asks that industry members:

1) use general guidelines, included in the RIAA memorandum, to determine whether a recording warrants a parental advisory label;
2) adopt a policy that the parental advisory label or other prominent notice of explicit content should appear in print advertising for explicit-labeled recordings and that advertising for explicit-content labeled recordings should not appear in publications, Web sites, or other commercial outlets whose primary (i.e., 50% or more) market demographic is 16 years of age or younger; and
3) adopt a policy that the parental advisory label should appear prominently in online retail sites in all stages of the transaction.

Marketing of Music Records

Information submitted by the recording companies shows that they market their explicitcontent labeled recordings at two levels. First, they advertise and market their recordings directly, assuming responsibility for the design of the materials and the dissemination of the promotions in a variety of venues, including print, broadcast and cable television, in-store displays, radio airplay, music videos, "street marketing," artist appearances on cable music television programming, and contests on Internet Web sites. Second, they promote music recordings through cooperative advertising agreements with retailers, wholesalers, and other distributors of music. Marketing efforts often begin several weeks before the release of a recording and can continue long after.

The Commission's review of marketing documents indicates that the recording companies often market explicit-content labeled recordings to a wide demographic, including a significant under-17 audience. Fifteen of the 55 marketing plans (27%) the Commission studied expressly identified teenagers as part of the group to which the companies planned on marketing the explicit recordings. Examples of express statements regarding the recordings' target audience include:

> "Target audience: Hip-Hop, Crossover, Pop, Male/ Female - 14-34" "Target audience: Alternative/urban, rock, pop, hardcore 12-34" "target demographic are 15-30 males and females of various ethnic backgrounds who are into hip hop."

"the 13-35 year old male demographic; which as we know is our target demo." Others more generally discuss promoting explicit recordings to "teens" and distributing materials at high schools or in popular teen venues.

Although the marketing documents for the remaining 40 explicit-content labeled recordings did not expressly set forth the age of the target audience, they detailed the same methods of marketing as the plans that specifically identified teens as a part of their target audience, including placing advertising in media that would reach a majority or substantial percentage of children under 17.

1. *Print advertising:* The recording companies routinely use print advertising to promote their explicit-content labeled recordings to children under 17. The marketing materials for 39 out of 55 labeled recordings (70%) discussed placing ads in magazines with a majority or significant teen audience (such as Blaze, GamePro, Metal Edge, Right On!, Seventeen, Skateboarding, Thrasher, Vibe, and YM). These magazines have an under-18 readership of between 40 and 80%. The recording companies also encouraged and closely tracked the placement in these publications of feature stories about their artists who had released explicit-content labeled recordings. The marketing plans for 11 explicit-content labeled recordings indicated that such features were scheduled to run in publications with a majority or substantial teen audience. In addition, the Commission reviewed the music advertising in recent issues of nine magazines with a majority or substantial teen readership audience and found ads for explicitcontent labeled recordings in each magazine.

2. *Television promotions - cable music channels:* Television cable channels that show music videos and other music-related programming figure prominently in the marketing of explicit-content labeled recordings to children under 17. The marketing plans almost

uniformly discuss airing music videos and placing advertisements and promotions on three music cable channels - MTV, BET, and/or The Box - all of which target and reach viewers between the ages of 12 and 34. The recording companies' marketing materials show that these companies often:

— advertise the release of labeled recordings during cable music programming;

— submit for airplay music videos of songs that appear on labeled recordings;

— encourage appearances by the artist on cable music programs; and

— arrange promotional activities with cable music channels, such as contests and special features on the artist. In addition, many of the marketing documents discuss securing promotions on specific cable music programs that appear during popular after-school and early-prime-time shows, such as MTV's Total Request Live and Jams Countdown and BET's Rap City. A review of these cable programs confirms that advertisements for labeled recordings, and music videos for songs from these recordings, appear on these channels during after-school and prime-time hours.

3. *Other television advertisements* : The marketing materials for the music recordings placed significantly less emphasis on network and non-music cable television advertising than did the plans for motion pictures.

Nonetheless, several of the marketing plans indicated that the recording companies intended to advertise and promote explicit-content labeled recordings on television programs with large under-17 audiences, such as The Simpsons, South Park, Buffy the Vampire Slayer, and various wrestling programs.

4. *Internet marketing:* The Commission found that Internet advertising and promotion is an integral part of most of the marketing plans for explicit recordings.. There is every indication that the companies will continue to increase their marketing of labeled recordings over the Internet: as one marketing plan noted, "Internet marketing and promotions is the wave of the future." Such marketing efforts easily reach a young audience, and surveys of teens indicate that a significant percentage of children are listening to music on and obtaining music from Internet Web sites.

Promoting a labeled recording over the Internet usually involves setting up an artist Web site or Web page (as part of a recording company site) where consumers can listen to short samples of songs (audio clips) from explicit recordings. These sites link to others, including artists' sites, and recording company and retail sites, from which recordings can be previewed, ordered, or downloaded. The recording companies also promote explicit-content labeled recordings through popular music sites, including mtv.com, bet.com, launch.com, and ubl.com. Several of the marketing plans for labeled recordings also detailed their use of electronic mail to alert fans about upcoming releases. Children under 17 constitute a significant percentage of the audience on these music Web sites.

5. *Street marketing:* Most of the marketing materials the Commission examined included plans to promote explicit-content labeled recordings through the use of aggressive "street marketing campaigns." The

companies use "street teams" to distribute a variety of promotional materials at non-traditional venues such as concerts, sporting goods stores, street fairs, and trendy clothing stores. The promotional materials involved include "coming soon" banners, posters, postcards, window displays, flyers, cassette and CD samplers, locker posters, key chains, t-shirts, hats, pencils, baseball cards, CDs, and "scratch and win" promotions. Street marketing efforts also include outdoor advertising for labeled recordings on billboards, posters at bus shelters, bus stop benches, buildings, and street poles. Several plans discussed attaching promotions for the labeled recordings to public buses, ice cream trucks, and shuttle vans that drive through urban neighborhoods.

In efforts geared specifically to the under-17 audience, several plans discussed distributing promotional materials for, and playing music and music videos from, explicit recordings in sporting goods and apparel stores popular with teens, such as Foot Action and Downtown Locker Room.One plan also discussed distributing singles from a labeled recording for play at "Back To High School" parties.

6. *Radio:* Radio is an important medium for reaching the youth market. Many of the marketing documents the Commission reviewed described plans to seek heavy radio play of singles from explicit-content labeled recordings on radio stations with a primary audience of 12- to 24-yearolds. These documents emphasized placings ads and other promotions, such as concert ticket giveaways, album giveaways, and a variety of prize promotion contests, on these stations. In addition, several of the marketing plans provided for on-air artist interviews on these stations.

7. *Licensing:* Like the motion picture and electronic game companies, the recording companies often cross-market their products through licensing agreements. The companies agree to the use of songs from explicit-content labeled recordings in other products marketed to teens, such as movies, video games, and television programs. Several companies licensed songs from labeled albums for use in R-rated movies that the movie studios promoted to an audience of 12- to 17-year-olds. One company licensed music from explicit-labeled recordings for use in PG and PG-13 movies.

The recording companies also licensed music from explicit-content labeled recordings for use in electronic games. One company licensed music from labeled recordings for use on a "fighting" game rated M ("Mature" audiences) that marketing documents indicated was targeted to 12- to 24-year-olds. Two companies approved the use of music from explicit-content labeled recordings on E-rated ("Everyone") video games. Further, the companies provided agreements authorizing the use of music from labeled recordings in programs and networks popular with teens. One marketing plan detailed a cross-marketing effort involving a contest with a clothing company whose products are "targeted to men and women 12-24," and also discussed using the contest as a means to "gather tens of thousands of e-mail addresses."

Retailing of Music Recordings

Recordings with an explicit content label are sold at specialty music stores, large electronics retailers, department stores, and on the Internet, among other locations. The eight music retailers the Commission contacted take a variety of approaches toward selling labeled recordings. Of the six of these music retailers with "bricks and mortar" stores:

— Two have company-wide policies restricting the purchase of labeled recordings in their retail stores by the age of the purchaser. One has a written policy not to sell any labeled CDs to "children," which some individual stores within the chain define as anyone age 17 and under. The other said its policy is not to sell recordings that display the advisory label to anyone under 13 years of age without a parent or guardian present.

— Three do not place any restrictions on in-store purchases of explicit recordings by children of any age.

— One does not carry recordings with a parental advisory label in its stores, stocking only the edited versions of these recordings.

Seven of the eight retailers contacted by the Commission sell explicit music on their Web sites; none imposes any age restrictions on online purchasers of explicit music.

The undercover shopper study conducted for the Commission confirms that retail stores rarely restrict children from purchasing explicit-labeled music. In that survey of 383 music stores, unaccompanied children ages 13-16 were able to buy an explicit-content labeled recording 85% of the time. Moreover, only about 12% of the music stores posted information about the parental advisory system or about the store's sales policy regarding explicit-content labeled recordings.

Electronic Game Industry Self-regulatory System

Beginning in the early 1990's, Congress responded to concern about the violent content in some electronic games with hearings and legislative proposals. Although no legislation was enacted, several members of Congress were critical of the electronic game industry for its lack of a self-regulatory system to rate electronic games. In 1994, industry members formed the Interactive Digital Software Association ("IDSA") to address this criticism. The IDSA, in turn, created and funded a separate division, the Entertainment Software Rating Board ("ESRB"), to develop an interactive software rating system to assist parents in their efforts to select appropriate games for their children.

The IDSA/ESRB system rates game software published for all gaming platforms, including cartridgebased and CD-based console systems (such as the Nintendo 64, the Sega Dreamcast, and the Sony Playstation, which hook up to a television set) and personal computer-based systems (such as a Windowsbased Windowsbased PC or a Macintosh). The ESRB's rating symbol can be found on all console-based video games and on nearly all personal computer software games.

The electronic game industry's self-regulatory system is the most comprehensive of the three industry systems studied by the Commission. It is widely used by industry members and has been revised repeatedly to address new challenges, developments, and concerns regarding the practices of its members. Its requirements are set out in the IDSA's Advertising Code of Conduct ("Adcode"), first adopted in 1995, and in the ESRB's Principles and Guidelines for Responsible Advertising Practices ("Ad Principles"), which became effective in January 2000.

To evaluate the electronic game industry's self-regulatory system, the Commission obtained information from the IDSA and the ESRB concerning the development and enforcement of the self-regulatory mechanisms they established for industry members. To assess industry members' use of those self-regulatory mechanisms, the Commission contacted 11 video and personal computer game publishers and obtained marketing and media plans for over 200 games that the ESRB had rated as containing violent content, including plans for most of the best-selling Mature-rated games from the last three years.

According to the ESRB, each electronic game title is rated by three people who have no ties to industry and whose identities remain anonymous to industry members. The rating panel for any given game title is selected from a pool of more than 200 individuals with different demographic characteristics; members of the pool vary by gender, ethnicity, age, and marital and parental status. Each three-member panel rates a game based on materials submitted by the game publisher or developer, typically videotaped footage of the most extreme portions of the game. During the review, each rater records every instance in which he or she observes a segment of gameplay that qualifies under a particular content rating category. When at least two of the three raters apply the same rating category to the same segment of the game, that rating category becomes the consensus rating for the game.

The IDSA/ESRB system rates game titles according to five age-based categories: (1) Early Childhood, or "EC"; (2) Everyone, or "E";199 (3) Teen, or "T"; (4) Mature, or "M"; and (5) Adults Only, or "AO." By definition, game titles rated M contain content suitable only for persons ages 17 and older, and T-rated titles contain content suitable only for persons ages 13 and older. There is also a Rating Pending category ("RP") to indicate that a game has been submitted to, but not yet rated by, the ESRB.201 According to the ESRB, nearly 75% of games have been rated either EC or E, while 19% have a T rating, 7% have an M rating, and less than 1% have an AO rating.

As in the motion picture rating system, a descriptive phrase may be assigned to the letter rating to indicate content that might be of concern to parents, such as language, sexual themes, or violence. Descriptors reflecting violent content include "Mild Animated Violence,""Mild Realistic Violence," "Comic Mischief," "Animated Violence," "Realistic Violence," "Animated Blood and Gore," "Realistic Blood and Gore," "Animated Blood," and "Realistic Blood." The clear majority of games, such as sports and racing games or strategy and puzzle games, do not contain graphic violence or depict blood and gore.

Yet hundreds of games do, and, due to technological advances, it is now possible for the maiming and killing depicted in those games to be inflicted with a vast array of weaponry and illustrated in graphic, near lifelike detail. The descriptors, however, do not indicate the intensity of violence in a game. All the violence descriptors but two - "Animated Blood and Gore" and "Realistic Blood and Gore" - may appear in E-rated games. Games rated T, M, or AO may be assigned any of the violence descriptors. Although the M-rating may suggest a greater level of violence compared to T- and E-rated games, the particular game may have received the M-rating for content other than violence (e.g., strong sexual content). Thus, although the descriptors, when combined with the ratings, do provide parents with information that is helpful in making decisions as to what is appropriate for their children, the degree of violence may not always be apparent.

Requirements for Packaging, Advertising, and Marketing

a. *Disclosure of rating information on product packaging and in advertising:* Unlike the film and music industries, the electronic game industry requires the display of rating icons and, in most cases, content descriptors on packaging, in print ads, and online. It also requires television ads to include a voice-over stating the game's rating. Specific requirements include:

— display of the rating icon on the front of the package and any content descriptors on the back;

— display of the rating icon on all game cartridges, compact discs, and floppy disks;

— display of the rating icon and content descriptors in print advertisements;

— display of the rating icon and a voice-over of the rating in televison ads; and

— display of the rating icon on game Web sites and on pages where a game "demo" or trailer is accessed, and display of the rating icon and content descriptors on product ordering pages.

Although the Adcode expressly includes banner ads on Web sites within its very broad definition of online advertising, it does not require that banner ads contain either rating icons or content descriptors. Nor does the IDSA Adcode cover ads for products related to electronic games, such as action figures or other products licensed by game manufacturers.

The Commission reviewed product packaging, recent print and television advertising, and industry Web sites promoting particular games to assess industry compliance with the disclosure requirements. The review found a high level of compliance with the packaging requirements and with requirements concerning proper visual disclosure of the rating and voice-overs of rating information in television ads. Industry compliance was mixed, however, with respect to the requirement to display ratings and content descriptors in print advertising, although it appears that compliance levels are improving.

Compliance with the rating disclosure requirements for industry Web sites was poor. Although most sites complied with the basic requirement to display the ESRB rating, many failed to display the rating icon on pages where a demo could be downloaded or viewed, and only a few displayed required descriptors at the point where one could order a game.

To its credit, the IDSA has taken several steps to encourage industry members to comply with these requirements. It has contacted many individual game publishers regarding their noncompliance with the rating display requirements for packaging, print, and television advertising. For packaging violations, the IDSA has asked the violator to place a hold on any future shipments of games with noncompliant packaging and to distribute stickers containing the correct rating information for retailers to apply on any packaging already in stores.

For advertising violations, the IDSA has generally asked the publisher to avoid future noncompliance. None of the documents submitted to the Commission revealed an instance when a violation resulted in a fine or a revocation of the ESRB rating, which the IDSA has the power to seek. Even though most advertisements and packaging comply with the requirements to display rating information, consumer familiarity with and usage of the IDSA/ESRB system appear to be low.

According to the Commission's May-June 2000 survey of parents and children, 61% of parents were aware of a rating system for video games, but only 37% had both heard of and had more than slight familiarity with the rating system. A bare majority of parents who claimed to be aware of and at least slightly familiar with the rating system said they use the rating at least some of the time when their children want to play a video game.

However, just over half of those parents could correctly state that the rating system provides for both age-based ratings and content descriptors, and less than half could name a single one of the ESRB ratings unaided or distinguish the ESRB ratings from rating terminology used in the music or motion picture industries.

Other studies have demonstrated similarly low levels of familiarity and use. An ESRBsponsored survey of parents in 1999 found that 45% were aware of the electronic game rating system, in contrast with 94% of respondents for the movie rating system and 60% for the music labeling system.

A 1999 survey commissioned by the Kaiser Family Foundation found that about 53% of parents reported using ratings on electronic games. A smaller survey conducted by the National Institute on Media and the Family in 1998 suggested a lower level of use, finding that 40% of parents routinely looked at industry ratings before buying or renting computer or video games. At the same time, the game rating system appears to be helpful to those parents who actually use it. The Commission's study found that five in six of those parents who use the video game rating system at least some of the time when their children want to play a game were "very satisfied" or "somewhat satisfied" with the rating system.

Similarly, the Kaiser Survey reported that about 86% of parents who had used the rating system found it to be "very useful" or "somewhat useful." Eighty percent of respondents in the ESRB survey who had the components of the IDSA/ESRB system described to them found the system "very helpful" or "somewhat helpful."

As to violence, the Commission's survey found that a majority of parents who are at least slightly familiar with the system believe that the rating system does either an excellent (4%) or good (50%) job of informing parents about the level of violence in video games. In contrast, a Gallup poll conducted in June 1999 reported that 74% of respondents felt that the electronic game industry did not provide parents with enough information about violent content to make decisions about what is appropriate for children, while 20% believed that the information was sufficient.However, respondents in that poll apparently were not screened for experience with the system.

b. *Limits on violent content in advertising:* The IDSA/ ESRB system also governs the content of advertising. In the fall of 1999, the IDSA created the Advertising Review Council ("ARC") as a separate division of the ESRB. In addition to being given responsibility to enforce the Adcode, as of January 31, 2000, ARC became responsible for implementing, administering, and enforcing an expanded set of Principles and Guidelines for Responsible Advertising Practices ("Ad Principles"), which add new requirements beyond the Adcode to assist companies in providing for "responsible, appropriate, truthful and accurate advertising." Companies that receive an ESRB rating agree to comply with the Ad Principles and to cooperate with all of ARC's reviews, investigations, and inquiries. The IDSA charged ARC with ensuring that industry ads comply with the following four principles. An advertisement should:

— accurately reflect the nature and content of the game and the rating issued;

— not glamorize or exploit the ESRB rating;

— be created with a sense of responsibility towards the public; and

— not contain any content that may cause serious or widespread offense to the average consumer.

With regard to the violent content of ads, ARC will examine, among other things, whether ad copy includes graphic and/or excessive depictions of violence. Because the Ad Principles only recently took effect, ARC's initial efforts to foster compliance have focused principally on educating members about their requirements. Nonetheless, the Commission's review of recent ads in game enthusiast magazines shows several instances of ad copy for M-rated games that might be covered by these Principles, such as an ad that states, "the huge 15 foot genetically engineered Behemoth rips the cop's heart out and like a rag doll tosses his lifeless body across the room" or an ad that promises "more powerful weapons" and urges gamers to "exercise your trigger finger."

It is not clear whether ARC or the IDSA would consider these examples to violate the letter or spirit of the Ad Principles. ARC officials expect that compliance with the Ad Principles will be enhanced by the decision of leading game enthusiast magazine publishers to incorporate the Ad Principles into their ad acceptance practices. It remains to be seen, however, whether the game magazines will be effective in screening out excessive violence from game ads.

c. *Limits on marketing to minors:* Unlike the movie and music recording industries, the electronic game industry does prohibit marketing targeted to children under the age suggested in the game's rating. Since 1995, the IDSA Adcode has barred industry members from "specifically target(ing) advertising . . . for entertainment software products rated Teen, Mature, or Adults Only to consumers for whom the product is not rated as appropriate." According to the IDSA, this provision is intended to prohibit a company from advertising a game rated Teen or Mature in, for example, the Barbie Magazine. In a 1998 letter, the IDSA emphasized that the "anti-targeting provision is important to the integrity of the rating system and is meant to ensure that young people are not encouraged to play games that are not suitable for them."

Marketing Electronic Games

Publishers of electronic games rely heavily on print advertising, especially in gaming enthusiast magazines, and make frequent use of Internet and television advertising to promote new game titles. Other promotional tactics used by one or more industry members include: instore displays at major game and toy retailers; the giveaway of sampler or "demo" disks of the game in popular gaming magazines; the aggressive solicitation of online and print press coverage, particularly for previews, reviews, and magazine covers; the creation of "official" Web sites or Web pages for a game title where browsers can learn about the game, view game clips, or download an abbreviated version of the game; the encouragement of electronic chat about the game on the Internet; direct mail and e-mail solicitations; "street marketing" (the distribution of posters, flyers, and stickers at clubs, music shops, and skateboard shops); the giveaway of game-related paraphernalia, such as sunglasses, stickers, t-shirts, and key chains; and game giveaways over the radio.

The Commission's review of industry documents indicates that nearly all the game companies contacted have marketed violent M-rated games to children in violation of the IDSA's anti-targeting provision. These violations are evidenced foremost by marketing documents for M-rated games that expressly target children (typically boys) under age 17. This under-17 targeting occurred as late as February 2000, the cut-off date for Commission-requested materials.

The marketing documents provided to the Commission indicate that at least 83 of the 118 violent M-rated games studied (70%) were targeted to children under 17. Sixty of the 118 game titles (51%) had at least one plan that expressly included children under 17 in the game's target audience. The incidence of express targeting was much higher for console games (72%) than for personal computer games (26%).

Marketing documents for 23 other M-rated games, though they did not expressly identify children under 17 as the target audience, included plans to advertise the games in magazines or on television shows with a majority or substantial under-17 audience, strongly suggesting that children under 17 were being targeted. Overall, 10 of the 11 companies contacted by the Commission (91%) produced at least one marketing document expressly identifying males (denoted by the letter "M") under 17 as the core, primary, or secondary target of their advertising campaigns for a violent M-rated game.

In nearly all these instances, males over age 17 were also part of the target audience. Most of the plans targeting an under-17 audience set age 12 as the younger end of the target spectrum, e.g:, "M 12-17" or "M 12-24," but two targeted children as young as six and eight. In several instances, company marketing documents contained inconsistent statements on whether the game's target audience included children under age 17. For example, a 1999 creative brief for a violent M-rated game stated, "The ad campaign MUST be targeted to people over the age of 17. . . . No GUNS or BLOOD should appear anywhere in the ads. . . . Rating icon to be prominent in all ads." At the same time, the marketing and media plans for the game expressly targeted a 12- to 17-year-old audience and planned advertisements in magazines and during television shows highly popular with younger teens.

Further, while some marketing plans indicated an intent to market M-rated games to an older audience, others targeted under-17 consumers while simultaneously acknowledging that this practice might conflict with the game's M rating. For example, a 1997 plan stated, in part:

Although Nintendo 64 purchasers space a large range in terms of age (6-34 years old), we recommend approaching the middle segment of this group because: [The game] has an M rating, which 1) may discourage parents from buying the game, and 2) hinder clearance of a commercial airing in shows primarily for children under 12. However, the younger the audience, the more likely they are to be influenced by TV advertising. Therefore, the recommended media target audience is: Males 12-17 - Primary Males 18-34 - Secondary.

In addition, two plans for games developed in 1998 described the target market as "Males 17-34 due to M rating (the true target is males 12-34) who own, or plan to own a PSX machine," and "Target: Males 17-34 due to M rating (the true target is M9-34) who own or plan to buy an N64 machine." Aside from express statements targeting an under-17 audience, the marketing documents show plans to place advertisements for M-rated games:

1) in magazines with a majority or close to a majority under-17 audience;

2) on the television shows most popular with younger teens; and

3) on Internet sites popular with younger teens.

The documents also show that the planned/actual television and print advertising for M-rated games resulted in extensive exposure to those under age 17 (typically 12-17). The following chart provides an overview of the extent to which each of the companies contacted by the Commission appears to have targeted teens under 17 in their marketing of M-rated games.

The companies' efforts at targeting youngsters under 17 appear to have had some success. Although only 7% of video games are rated M, a variety of studies and surveys indicate that these games, despite their "Mature" rating, are quite popular with boys under 17. In a survey sponsored by the Commission, 24% of children between the ages of 11 and 16 included at least one M-rated game in their list of three favorite games. Data from industry surveys in 1998 and in 1999 indicate that 40% of users of the M-rated games included in those surveys were under 18. Information from game data registration from two companies is mixed, however. Data from one company indicate that for five of its M-rated games, 14% to 67% of the users were 17 and under, while data from another company indicate that for two of its M-rated games, 10% of the users were under age 18.

1. *Print advertising:* All but two of the companies produced marketing documents containing plans to place ads for M-rated games in magazines that have a majority under-17 readership. Specifically, nine of the 11 companies' marketing documents show repeated plans to place numerous ads for M-rated games in magazines such as GamePro, Electronic Gaming Monthly, Expert Gamer, Tips and Tricks, and the Unofficial PlayStation Magazine, all of which have a majority (from 54% to 68%) of readers or subscribers age 17 or under. The Commission reviewed 18 months (from January 1999 through June 2000) of two of those magazines - GamePro and Electronic Gaming Monthly. This review reveals that 16 industry members, including eight of the companies contacted by the Commission, advertised Mrated games in these magazines. Although one company placed only a single ad, others used these magazines more frequently, with five IDSA members placing 20 or more advertisements for M-rated games. In fact, the 16 companies collectively placed more than 200 advertisements for M-rated games in these magazines, even though 60% of their readership is 17 and under, indicating broad-based targeting that is inconsistent with the self-regulatory system. A breakout of the magazine ads by rating is pesented below.

2. *Television advertising:* Game companies also use television advertising to target M-rated games to teen audiences. Marketing documents set out a long list of televison programs popular with teens ages 12 to 17 on which companies planned to place their

advertisements for M-rated games. These programs include The Simpsons, WWF Smackdown, That 70's Show, King of the Hill, Dawson's Creek, Buffy the Vampire Slayer, Xena: Warrior Princess, The Wayans Brothers, Hercules: The Legendary Journeys, Baywatch, X-Files, V.I.P., Smart Guy, and WCW Wrestling. Company documents also show plans for frequent ad placements for M-rated games on cable networks popular with teens: MTV, Comedy Central, Sci-Fi, USA, TBS (wrestling), and TNT (wrestling). Indeed, at least two companies' media plans for several M-rated games expressly singled out programming on these networks because of their "high M12-24 composition" or because they were "Youth-targeted." A few companies also planned television ads for shows airing in the afternoon, a time-frame particularly popular with teens.

3. *Internet marketing:* Many of the marketing documents describe plans to build game title awareness and generate sales through promotional efforts on the Internet and, in particular, at Web sites frequented by younger teens. Ten of the 11 companies (91%) produced marketing documents for M-rated games showing plans to place advertisements on popular teen Web sites.

Although the Commission's primary focus was M-rated games, the Commission also requested marketing documents for some games rated T (Teen) which contain descriptors for violence, and received information on approximately 85 such games. These documents reveal several instances in which company plans expressly targeted T-rated games to those under age 13, including, in two cases, children as young as six. Overall, however, game companies appeared to expressly target an underage audience far less frequently for T-rated games than they did for M-rated games. Six of the 11 (55%) companies produced at least one marketing document for a T-rated game that listed children under the age of 13 as the primary or secondary targets of the advertising campaign. Of the 41 T-rated games for which marketing or media plans specified a target age, 10 (24%) games had a plan that expressly included those under 13 in the target audience.

In many instances, the planned magazine and television advertising campaigns to promote these T-rated games looked much like those for many M-rated games, with plans to place ads in the same magazines and on the same television shows. In other instances, the planned programs and publications skewed younger than those used to market M-rated games. For example, marketing documents from two companies revealed plans to advertise three Teen games on either the Cartoon Network, Nickelodeon, or both; a large majority of the audience for these channels is between the ages of two and 11. Other plans suggested ad placement on several print publications popular with young children - DC Comics-Kids, Sports Illustrated for Kids, Nickelodeon Magazine, and Disney Adventures.

Company documents frequently reference plans to use or license images or characters from M- or T-rated games in a wide variety of products, including action figures, comic books, tshirts, stickers, key chains, posters, mouse pads, sweatshirts, caps, decals, temporary tatoos, and hand-held versions of the game. As noted above, the IDSA Adcode does not expressly cover licensing.

One area that has drawn particular criticism is game licensees' marketing to children of action figures based on characters from popular M-rated games. Sold in the toy aisles of major mass merchandisers and in toy stores, these action figures - regardless of the rating of the game on which the figure is based - are labeled as suitable for children, sometimes as young as four or five. For example, the package for one action figure based on a violent M-rated game states prominently on the front, "Ages 4 and up." The back of the package invites the reader to "[j]oin the blood battle" by playing the Nintendo 64 version of the game, which is M-rated. As an additional incentive to purchase the game, the package offers free game codes for navigating the M-rated version of the game.

Action figures, however, also may appeal to older collectors, and comic book retailers catering to adults may stock action figures in the collectibles area of their stores. Several magazine and Web sites target collectors, with ads offering "retired" action figures at premium prices. Perhaps in response to such criticism, one game company licensor recently adopted a policy to require its licensees not to advertise, market, or sell products based on M-rated games to those under 17, and to include on product packaging a statement that such products are based on an M-rated game.

Another major licensee has begun labeling its licensed products that are based on M-rated games (and R-rated movies) as "Recommended for mature collectors." E. Retailing of Electronic Games The ESRB has urged retailers to adopt policies restricting the sale of Mature- and Adult Only-rated electronic games. In particular, the ESRB's "Commitment to Parents" program encourages electronic game retailers to prohibit the sale of computer and video games rated M to persons under the age of 17 without parental permission, and to refuse to sell games rated AO to persons under 18. To assess the extent of children's access to violent M-rated games, the Commission contacted 12 retailers and online sellers of electronic games. All of the electronic game retailers the Commission contacted carry M-rated games; a few, however, restrict the types of M-rated games stocked. For example, one retailer states that it has a policy not to carry M-rated titles that contain certain content descriptors, including "Realistic Blood & Gore." Another retailer has opened several stores that do not carry games with mature or adult content in order to cater specifically to children. Most of the retailers contacted do not carry AO-rated games.

The ESRB indicates that four retailers have agreed to make their best efforts not to sell games rated "Mature" to children under 17, and that the ESRB is giving each store that participates a certificate it can post announcing that it has made a "Commitment to Parents." One of these four retailers uses a point-of-purchase cash register system that prompts the cashier, whenever the bar code for an M-rated game is scanned into the system, either to ask for age identification if the customer appears to be under 17 or to inform the adult purchaser that the product is intended for a mature audience.

A fifth retailer has adopted a policy of not renting or selling M-rated electronic games to youths under the age of 17 unless parental consent is given. None of the retailers contacted specifically requests age information before completing an Internet purchase, even where it has policies to verify age for in-store purchases. At least one retailer relies, instead, on its credit-card-only purchase policies to restrict children from buying inappropriate games. The undercover shopper survey of electronic game retailers conducted for the Commission demonstrates that children under 17 can easily buy M-rated games.

Juvenile Justice Act

In USA, the Juvenile Justice Act implements a comprehensive strategy aimed at addressing the problem of juvenile violence. The legislation devotes substantial resources to state and local governments for the continued development and implementation of innovative and effective accountability and prevention programs. The legislation also targets the growing national problem of criminal street gangs, which frequently lure juveniles into illicit activity, and it works to keep firearms and explosives out of the hands of children.

Equally important, the act begins to confront what experts consider a principal cause of juvenile violence: depictions of violence in the media. The relevant provisions, summarized below, seek to reduce children's exposure to media violence by encouraging corporate responsibility and empowering parents.

In the spirit of limited self-government, corporate responsibility is best spurred through moral suasion, not government compulsion. This approach, reflected in the Juvenile Justice Act, has the added advantage of emphatically respecting the First Amendment traditions. In the Internet industry, Steve Case, chairman of America Online, has agreed to take steps to limit the access of children to violent video games on the Internet. And from the music business, BMG President and CEO Strauss Zelnick's views stand as the model we urge others to emulate: "There is no question that the First Amendment would allow us to do whatever we want, but I believe we are all editors, and editors have a social responsibility and responsibility to themselves to decide what they want to publish. . . . There's clearly a line that we won't cross."

Industry Ratings Enforcement

The legislation provides for the voluntary cooperation of the entertainment industries to develop, implement, and enforce voluntary programming guidelines to remove harmful influences on children. The legislation provides a limited exemption from antitrust laws that enables the relevant industries to conduct joint discussions and enter into agreements to develop voluntary guidelines and ensure retail compliance with existing ratings and labeling systems.

Media Campaign Against Youth Violence

The bill provides for a 2-year national media campaign against youth violence. This campaign, for which the Senate has authorized $25 million, will be developed in consultation with national, statewide, and community-based youth organizations, including the Boys and Girls Clubs of America.

Restrict Access to Federal Property for Production of Violent Media

The act restricts the use of federal property, equipment, or personnel for filming motion pictures or television shows for commercial purposes that glorify or endorse violence.

Parental Empowerment Through Internet Screening

This measure brings the V-Chip concept to the Internet. Internet service providers will be required to offer screening/filtering technology that enables parents to limit their children's access to material on the Internet. Parents can use these tools to block access to on-line content and web sites they deem unsuitable for their children. Many in the Internet industry deserve praise for already moving to develop and distribute this technology.

Studies and Reports

The legislation also provides for further studies concerning media violence and establishes a national commission that will, with the help of parents and children, identify the causes of youth violence.

National Institute of Health Study

The study will explore the impact of violent video games and music on child development and youth violence. The study will eliminate a gap in existing research, which to date has focused largely on the impact of television and film. It is worthless to await the results of this study before taking action to address these forms of media violence. Existing research suggests that violent music lyrics have the same deleterious effect on the youth as television and film violence. And as for video games and the Internet, experts predict that the interactive nature of the violence will cause even more harm than these other media forms.

Federal Trade Commission/Attorney General Joint Study

The legislation provides for a joint study of the marketing practices of the motion picture, recording, and video/ personal computer game industries. The study, like previous studies directed at the practices of the tobacco industry, will focus on the marketing of violent or sexually explicit material to minors, and on whether retail merchants, movie theaters, and others have policies to keep minors away from these harmful products. In carrying out this study the FTC and the Attorney General are authorized to subpoena marketing plans and internal memoranda to determine to what extent these industries are pushing violence to the youth.

National Youth Violence Commission

Finally, the act establishes a National Youth Violence Commission which will conduct a comprehensive factual study of incidents of youth violence to determine the root causes of youth violence. The Commission, comprising 16 members, will examine, among other things, the effect on youth of depictions of violence in the media. In fulfilling its mandate, the Commission may hold hearings, take testimony from parents and students, and subpoena information. The Commission will report its findings to the President and Congress.

Proposals for Further Action

While the Juvenile Justice Act represents a promising start, much more needs to be done to reduce media violence. Further steps should be animated by the two imperatives that underlie the Juvenile Justice Act: encouraging corporate responsibility and empowering parents. Many media executives appear sincere in expressing their concerns about media violence. Thus, absent signs that this optimistic view of the industry is mistaken, policy proposals should facilitate, rather than compel, the exercise of corporate responsibility. As for parents, it bears repeating that they remain the most promising allies in this effort. Public policy initiatives therefore must empower them to fulfill their protective responsibilities.

National Media Campaign to Educate Parents

The effectiveness of V-Chips, Internet filters, rating systems and the like depend on the ability and willingness of parents to use those devices.Recent studies conducted by the Annenberg Public Policy Center at the University of Pennsylvania have revealed that parents' knowledge of the V-Chip and the related television rating symbols is actually declining. This lack of knowledge likely explains why 62% of parents reported that they had not used the age-based rating system in selecting what their children watched on television.

Congress should direct and implement a national media campaign, similar to those used for drugs, smoking, and drunk driving prevention, to educate parents about the tools at their disposal. This campaign, which would be administered by the Department of Justice's Office of Juvenile Justice and Delinquency Prevention, would make use of all forms of media.

National Parents' Clearinghouse on Children and Entertainment Violence

Congress should establish a national clearinghouse on children and entertainment violence, which could be modeled on the National Clearinghouse for Alcohol and Drug Information. The clearinghouse would provide material on the following topics, among others: the ways that children learn violence, how to select appropriate toys, how to teach children anger management and conflict resolution skills, and ways that parents can teach their values to their children.

Disclosure of Music Lyrics

A primary policy goal must be to empower parents to shield their children from harmful media influences. Empowerment often means simply ensuring that parents have ready access to relevant information. For instance, parents frequently complain that, with respect to the music their children buy, parents are unable to screen the lyrics beforehand. Consideration should be given to a proposal that would require retail establishments that sell music to make the lyrics of any album, compact disc, tape, or other medium available for on-site parental review.

Use of Government Facilities

The Juvenile Justice Act contains a provision that will restrict the use of federal property, equipment, or personnel for filming motion pictures or television shows for a commercial purpose that glorifies or endorses violence. Encouragement, through financial incentives, should be given to those who would use federal property, equipment, or personnel to create films or programs suitable for children. To that end, relevant federal agencies should make those items available at reduced rates to individuals or entities who would make such use of them.

Internet Hate Ban

The proliferation of messages of hate and violence on the Internet raises the possibility that federal legislation is needed to protect impressionable youth from such material. Any such legislation should accomplish two objectives:

(1) encourage Internet service providers to rid their systems of material intended to incite a person to commit an act of violence, and

(2) proscribe, under penalty of criminal prosecution, the posting of such material on the Internet, when posted with the intent to incite an act of violence.

Parental Empowerment and Guidance

While government can play an important role in ending youth violence, we can agree with the wisdom expressed by Representative Henry Hyde, the Chairman of the House Judiciary Committee: "Parents ultimately bear the responsibility for the environment in which their children are raised. We can pass laws to keep this garbage out of the hands of kids, but parents have to guide their children away from the polluting environment the greedy purveyors of violence are eager to sell." Yet too many parents lack the necessary information to guide their children away from violent media.

Internet Screening and Other High-Tech Tools

The proliferation of personal computers and the Internet pose daunting new challenges to parents. Unlike other forms of media, the Internet, with its constantly changing content, does not lend itself easily to a rating system. What is more, the efforts of parents to block objectionable content are often frustrated by their children's computer prowess. Not surprisingly, many parents view the Internet as both a blessing and a curse. Yet, parents do have at their disposal numerous tools to shield children from Internet content they find unsuitable. First, and most basic, parents can place the household computer in a common area frequented by other family members. In this way a child's curiosity would be tempered by a fear of detection.

Parents can also seek a technological fix. Software filters exist that allow parents to block sexual or violent content, restrict their children's e-mail, limit the amount of time children spend over the Internet, and track the Internet sites they visit. Parents can obtain many of these filters on the Internet. In addition, web browsers are available that integrate filtering features. Finally, parents should check with their Internet Service Providers, many of which provide parental filters.

A helpful development in this area is the creation of rating systems for Internet sites and games. Perhaps the most promising is a system based on the one described above for packaged video games. This system, developed in 1997 by the ESRB (the same entity that rates video games), uses the same 5 age-based rating labels ("EC", "E", "T", "M", and "AO") for "contained" sites that do not allow interaction between the site and the user or exchange of content or other information that could influence suitability of use.

For interactive sites that provide opportunities for the user to engage in an interactive experience, the system assigns the same labels, except that each label is followed by the letter "I" (thus, "ECI", "EI", "TI", "MI", and "AOI"). The "I" cautions that the user can exchange information with other users who may have differing or controversial opinions, or who may influence game play.

Like the video game rating system, the Internet rating system uses "descriptors" to further explain the content of Internet sites and games. As with the V-Chip and television ratings, filtering technology used in conjunction with the ESRB ratings will empower parents to shield their children from unsuitable material.

Practical Guidance for Parents

In 1996, the American Medical Association published a guide for parents interested in limiting the media's influence on their children. Among the Association's suggestions:

— Do not make the television the focal point of the house.

— Limit television use to one or two hours per day.

— Keep the television turned off during mealtimes (66% of American families have the television turned on during at least one meal a day), and keep televisions out of children's bedrooms.

— Do not use the television, videos, or video games as a baby sitter; set a good example by limiting your own television viewing.

Be alert to the shows and video games your children see. Watch what your children are watching and talk about the program while it is on. Some suggested questions to discuss with your children:

1) Where did the story take place?

2) Who are the characters? Are they always good or bad? Sometimes? When?

3) Do the characters remind them of anyone they know in real life?

4) What was the problem presented in the program?

5) How was the problem solved? Would the solution work in real life?

6) If the program contains violence:

    a) How do you think the victim feels?

    b) Did the television version of violence omit anything?

    c) What would happen if people did this in real life? Why?

    d) What would have been a way of solving the problem without anyone getting hurt?

    e) Did the characters think about alternatives before using violence as a way to solve the conflict?

Learn about movies that are playing and videos and video games available for rental or purchase? Be explicit with children about what is appropriate for them to see.

— Only watch television when there is something specifically worth watching.

— Be careful about what your child watches just before bedtime.

— Teach your children about advertising and the influence media has.

Set a good example, for children learn by your example. Warns child psychologist Lois Nightingale: "If children see parents watching 'Rambo,' then get 'Power Rangers' turned off, there are some incongruities there."

In August 1999, the American Academy of Pediatrics published a list of recommendations as part of its report on media education. While many of those recommendations mirror those of the American Medical Association listed above, others go even further in an effort to reduce the impact of media on children. For example:

— Children under 2 years old should not watch television.

— Parents should create an "electronic media-free" environment in all children's rooms.

— Pediatricians should begin incorporating questions about media use into their routine child health visits so that they can offer counsel and support.

— Pediatricians should alert and educate parents, children, adolescents, teachers, school officials, and other professionals about media-associated health risks.

Dr. Mark Griffith from the University of Plymouth has developed a checklist to help parents determine if their children are playing too many video games. The checklist asks if your child:

— plays video games most days?

— often plays for long periods of time?

— plays for excitement?

— gets restless if he cannot play?

— plays for a personal best?

— often tries unsuccessfully to limit playing?

— plays instead of doing his homework?

— sacrifices social activity?

According to Dr. Griffith, if the answers to more than 4 of these questions are "yes," your child may be playing video games excessively and parents should intervene and impose limits.

Parents should know that the impact on children of television, movies, music, video games, and the Internet arises not only from the kinds of behavior they promote, but also from the other activities they replace. A Canadian study analyzed the changes in how families living in a small town spent their days before and after television was introduced. The study found that after television became available, people spent less time talking, socializing outside the home, doing household tasks, engaging in leisure activities, and being involved in community activities. People even slept less once the television entered the home.

Parents should supply their children with alternatives to television, movies, music, video games, and the Internet. Regularly providing things such as art supplies, books to read, athletic activities, or outdoor excursions will reduce the number of arguments about what to watch on television and teach children how to enjoy a broader range of activities. Parents should realize that there is simply no substitute for close adult supervision of, and involvement in, the lives of their children. Parents must take time to learn what their children are viewing and playing.

7

Media Education

Media literacy education is at a watershed moment around the world. A growing number of countries are developing media education programs in their schools. Media educators from around the world are meeting more often to share curricula, research, and strategies. The most recent conference, Summit 2000, "Children, Youth and the Media: Beyond the Millennium," was held in Toronto, Canada in May 2000. Representatives from nearly 60 countries attended, making this the largest gathering of media educators in history. In 1998–99, the 29th General Conference of the United Nations Educational, Scientific and Cultural Organization (UNESCO) approved support for media education following up on UNESCO's first call for media education in Paris in November 1989. In April 1999, 41 invited representatives from 33 countries met in Vienna and made the following statement and recommendations:

Media education is the entitlement of every citizen, in every country in the world, to freedom of expression and the right to information and is instrumental in building and sustaining democracy. . . . Media education should be introduced wherever possible within national curricula as well as in tertiary, non-formal and lifelong education.

The Vienna Conference went on to state that media education:

— enables people to gain an understanding of the communication media used in their society and the way they operate and to acquire skills in using these media to communicate with others;

— ensures that people learn how to:

— analyze, critically reflect upon, and create media texts;

— identify the sources of media texts, their political, social, commercial and/or cultural interests, and their contexts;

— interpret the messages and values offered by media;

— select appropriate media for communicating their own messages or stories and for reaching their intended audience.

Many positive media literacy developments of today are worth noting. In addition to new organizations promoting media literacy, a growing number of states have added media literacy goals to their education standards. In a 1999 study with Frank Baker, then president of the Alliance for a Media Literate America, we found that 48 of the 50 states had one or more elements of media education in their core curricular frameworks. These frameworks contribute to a growing legitimacy for media education, which was not nearly so available or widespread only a few years ago. The 1999 study surprised us, as well as many other U.S.

media educators, in that so many states, working independently, had brought media education into their curricular frameworks. The findings speak to the ongoing zeitgeist that recognizes the great and growing need for media education.

The considerable presence of media analysis goals in the areas of health and consumer skills also surprised us. Seventy-four percent of states (37 states) now have media education elements in their health and consumer education frameworks. Ninety-four percent (47 states) have media education elements in English and language and communication arts frameworks, but only 60 percent (30 states) call for media elements in social studies, history, and civics.

The call for media education in the United States dates back to the 1950s and the 1970s, when many critical viewing programs were developed, if not back to 1916, when psychologist Hugo Munsterberg called for the serious study, in schools, of the new medium of film, which he called "The Photoplay."One of the significant developments in the history of U.S. media education occurred in December 1992 when the Aspen Institute brought 25 educators and activists together for a National Leadership Conference. The group established a definition of media education and a vision for developing it in U.S. education, stating that a media-literate person should be able to access, analyze, evaluate, and produce both print and electronic media.

The Aspen Group also proposed the following precepts:

— Media are constructed, and construct reality.

— Media have commercial implications.

— Media have ideological and political implications.

— Form and content are related in each medium, each of which has a unique aesthetic, codes, and conventions.

— Receivers negotiate meaning in media.

Media literacy involves critically analyzing media messages; evaluating sources of information for bias and credibility; raising awareness of how media messages influence people's beliefs, attitudes, and behaviors; and producing messages using different forms of media.

Children throughout the world spend an average of three hours each day watching television. At this rate, by the time they reach age 75 they will have spent nine years watching TV. In the United States, they will have spent two of those nine years watching television ads. When we add the number of hours young people spend watching movies, listening to music and radio, and surfing the Internet, they easily devote one-third to one-half of our waking lives to electronic media. Yet many schools still treat poetry, short stories, and the novel as the only forms of English expression worthy of study. As a result, most children are not media literate, so they are poorly equipped to engage actively and think critically about the very media that most affect their lives.

Although school systems throughout the United States are mandated to teach critical thinking, if the schools are not linking this skill to the media world in which so many students are spending upwards of six hours a day, they are leaving a potential gold mine unexplored.

Most anyone who has engaged in media literacy instruction knows that, before long, parents will report that their children are no longer watching television in the same way they did before. Indeed, parents often remark that after instruction in media literacy, their children constantly point out things while they watch movies or TV programs. They identify jump cuts, fades, and voiceovers. They detect bias and the power of words to shift meaning and of music to alter the viewer's mood.

Television viewing – which formerly involved relatively passive reception – now involves much more mental activity. Willingly, although without knowing it, the student is now spending a good chunk of those three hours of daily television viewing engaged in critical thinking. The same thing can happen when they are surfing the Net, listening to radio, watching movies, reading the newspaper, or playing video games. This is not to say that they will be engaged in critical analysis every moment, but they will be using their higher critical faculties much more if they have been given some of the basic tools of media literacy, of media analysis, than if they have not.

We know of no evidence that more critical\appraisal undermines one's enjoyment of television or film. To the contrary, understanding how television shows and film are made enhances enjoyment. In some cases, one's tastes may eventually run to less obvious or more sophisticated material, but there is no reason to expect that a media-literate person can't still enjoy the media and derive pleasure and information simultaneously. If schools want students to spend more time thinking critically and practicing critical thinking skills, then they are missing the boat if they are not teaching media literacy and using the media as a site for this critical analysis.

Applications of Media Literacy

Promoting Democray

Research has shown that media literacy activities in social studies classes significantly promote civic participation and increase regular newspaper readership among teenagers. With the incredible rise of the Internet and the unedited nature of many websites, students need more than ever to learn how to assess the validity and credibility of the information to which they are exposed.

Our political life became increasingly mediated in the middle of the last century, and now – certainly in campaigns and elections, and in day-to-day governance – the media could hardly be more crucial to how we view politicians and our leaders, and how we think about the critical issues of the day. Should we go to war? How will we protect the environment? Will we be taxed more or less? These and every other vital question in our democracy are raised and debated, often superficially, in the nation's media.

Politicians have become extraordinarily adept at using the media to their advantage. If their interests are in line with the nation's, this can result in effective government. But as often as not, well-intended or not, vast distortions take place in our public life that are partly a function of how our media systems operate.

To the degree that the media are used to propagandize or manipulate and therefore interfere with the public being well informed, we need media education to be part of our schools' civics and social studies classes. No student should leave high school without knowing the classic techniques of persuasion and propaganda, many of which have been taught for decades, but not to all students. Students should be able to recognize "namecalling," "bandwagon," and "glittering generalities" in the arguments they hear and read. But this is only the most basic of beginnings.

Promoting Health

Media literacy techniques are also being used increasingly in programs designed to promote health and prevent substance abuse among young people. Indeed, the American Academy of Pediatrics has concluded that media education represents "a simple, effective approach to combating the myriad of harmful media messages seen or heard by children and adolescents."

To address health threats to children and adolescents, the U.S. Department of Health and Human Services and the White House Office of National Drug Control Policy have advocated teaching critical analysis of advertisements and other media presentations that promote the use and abuse of tobacco, alcohol, and drugs.

A particularly useful health education assignment involves having groups of middle-school students produce a five-minute videotape on a health topic of their choice, for example, nutrition, exercise, safe sex, or alcohol, drug, or tobacco abuse. The final production is shown to the whole class, if not the whole school, or more widely via public access cable. Here's what often happens. First, students develop more interest in the research aspects of the project because they are responsible for making a public service announcement (PSA) for their peers and for the larger community. Compared with a written report that only the teacher will see, students making a PSA become very motivated to ensure that the information they convey is accurate.

The students learn organizational, research, writing, editing, and production skills. And guess whose PSA other students are more likely to pay attention to and learn from: the government's, the advertising council's, or the ones made by their peers? Such peerdriven media literacy health projects can really bring students alive and help make schoolwork more relevant.

Media literacy approaches can also be used in programs focused on conflict resolution and the reduction of aggression and violence. Middle or high school students can be asked, for example, to view part of a film depicting a growing conflict between two rival gangs in a school. The film is stopped, and the students are then assigned to groups to write the next scene, wherein the characters resolve the conflict through talk, rather than with fists, knives, or guns.

The assignment prompts students to think through how a conflict might be peaceably resolved. Then, in sharing their solutions, the class has the opportunity to hear a variety of solutions. This increases the likelihood that some of these solutions will be mentally available should students become involved in a similar conflict.

Character education and social and emotional learning goals, so important in contemporary education and society, can also be met through media education. Indeed, how would one carry out character education today without having young people think about the values being taught by the media that surround them? Media literacy lessons are readily integrated with the six "pillars" of character education: trustworthiness, respect, responsibility, fairness, caring, and citizenship. These lessons can help students become much more aware of the values being promulgated by the media relative to their own developing values and those of their family and community.

Now let's spend a moment considering what goals the Aspen Institute had in mind in stating that a medialiterate person ought to be able to access, analyze, evaluate, and produce media. Why those four verbs?

Access. With the rise of the Internet, access is more important than ever. Not only should students be able to access the World Wide Web, they should also receive instruction in how to assess the value and validity of websites in all areas, whether medical, political, or educational.

Now that most anyone can create their own website, a great deal of freedom has been accorded citizens who choose to use it. But with the freedom of the Internet comes a new and increasing demand on our educational systems and on caregivers to help young people use the Internet and all other media – critically and thoughtfully.

Analyze. Analysis involves being able to detect propaganda and to understand that people are always involved in the construction of media messages, and that nearly all media messages are designed to do something, whether it is to inform, entertain, or persuade. Young people and adults alike need to learn how the media construct our understandings of issues, products, people, gender and race, and whole nationstates. Indeed, one "law" of communication is that people are most impressionable and most easily persuaded when they know very little about the topic or issue at hand.

People's impressions of other countries and of other peoples are often heavily based in what they have seen, heard, or read in the media. It follows that how people feel about aiding or making war against another country or people rests substantially on political decisions and public opinion, both of which are remarkably influenced by what people know, or think they know, via the media.

Evaluate. For people to evaluate the media means learning to appraise the value of media products for themselves and for their society. This is arguably an even more subjective process than analysis, but it is no less important. Media literacy education ought to contribute to an individual's ability to determine the value of any given film, television program, or magazine or newspaper article.

We especially want to encourage students to become autonomous in their assessment of media and to develop their own modes of criticism, interpretation, and evaluation. We may wish to choose and supervise the media exposure of young children, but eventually parents and teachers have to let go and expect them to negotiate the increasingly complex media worlds they inhabit largely on their own. And just as there is no single, correct way to interpret all of literature, there is no single, correct way to interpret all of television or film. The goal of media education should be to provide a grounding on which students can better develop their own idiosyncratic responses.

As important as critical thinking, health, and democracy are, we should not forget that the media convey, or constitute, various forms of artistic expression. Thus, we also want students to become more sophisticated in their appreciation of art forms across all media. Indeed, the educational establishment must recognize that some film and television classics are works of substantial artistry, subtlety, and power.

One way to integrate media literacy with traditional literacy is to emphasize writing skills in students' scripts and in their critical reviews of films, TV programs, advertising, and websites. One way to increase students' interest in literature is to help them recognize that many of the same storytelling techniques used in the classics are also used in the popular programs and films with which they are already familiar.

Students already respond to foreshadowing in a television series like Malcolm in the Middle or a movie like Spiderman; they are often simply unaware that foreshadowing is a deliberate technique used to heighten suspense, drama, and irony. Knowing the terms and being able to apply them is more important than some might think. Knowing about foreshadowing, symbolism, character development, and other techniques used in literature and in film and television permits greater appreciation of the art forms.

Produce. Students should also be able to produce media. First, being able to create one's own media messages is extraordinarily empowering. Sometimes for the first time in their lives, students see that they, too, can participate in making art or news, a film, a television program, or a website that affects other people. Many students involved in a media production in middle or high school report that it was among the most exciting and motivating experiences of their years in school. Second, by producing media, students learn in a more personal and profound way that media messages are "constructed."

One can show students how the simplest edits in film or television can substantially change the meaning and emotional impact of a scene or of an entire story. Students can learn how easy it is to include or edit out a particular shot, or how the choice of music can make a huge difference in how the audience experiences a character, a moment in a story, or a whole group of people. Showing students these things is an important and necessary part of media literacy instruction, but even better is for the students to become involved in making editorial decisions of their own, deciding for themselves what to leave in or leave out and in what order to present material.

Consider what students learn in the following assignment. A group of 6th graders is assigned to make an audio story about the school's new principal. They are given tape recorders and told to go out and interview the principal, teachers, other students, staff, and custodians and then come back in a week to edit the material down to a three-minute story that will be played for the student body over the school's public address system. What will the students learn? First, they'll learn to sift through one or two hours of interviews to find the few minutes of material that they want to stitch together. They will learn that the vast majority of their raw material never finds its way into the final product. They will learn that they must decide which sound bite is best to include, as well as how long it should play, in what order, and with what narration setting it up. In a nutshell, they will learn how incredibly constructed all such media messages are –every radio or TV news story they hear or view for the rest of their lives.

Note that this assignment can be done with extraordinarily inexpensive and durable equipment. Handheld tape recorders can be purchased for under 20.

And an audio editing capability is as close as any tape player with two tape drives. One doesn't need a fully equipped studio or television cameras to involve students in media production.

One obstacle to more rapid acceptance of media education is that some educators remain convinced that the only area appropriate for formal study in English and language arts classes is literature. But there can be little question that the patina of time alone will eventually make the formal study of electronic media acceptable to educational traditionalists.

We can expect media education to become commonplace by the middle of this century, if not before. More than 2,300 years ago, Plato wrote that a "sound education consists in training people to find pleasure and pain in the right objects." But though most people now spend half their leisure time watching television and film, too few schools yet devote formal attention to helping students become more sophisticated media consumers. Most fundamentally, we need to encourage youth to take the media seriously, to understand where media messages come from and why messages are presented as they are and to what effect.

Prevention of public health problems

Today most prevention practitioners and researchers, as well as concerned teachers and parents, recognize that many of the messages we get from the media are risk factors for numerous public health problems. From the time we wake up to the radio alarm clock to the time we fall asleep with the TV on, we live in a media culture. We cannot escape the media's influence on either our healthy or unhealthy behaviors.

Numerous studies over the past five decades have examined the impact of media on children, with regard to such risky behaviors as violence; alcohol, tobacco, and other drug abuse; poor body image and eating disorders; precocious, unsafe sexual activity; and teen pregnancy. More than 1,000 studies have looked at the effects of violence in television and movies, including the three-year National Television Violence Study completed in 1998. Most of these studies conclude that children who watch significant amounts of television and movie violence are more likely than children who see less media violence to exhibit aggressive behavior, attitudes, and values.

A study of ninth graders in San Jose, California, found that increased television and music video viewing are risk factors for the onset of alcohol use in adolescents. The study recommended that attempts to prevent adolescent alcohol use should address the adverse influences of alcohol use in the media.

Another study found that seventh- and ninthgraders were more likely to approve of premarital sex after watching MTV for less than one hour. The media are so pervasive that youth, in particular, do not perceive their influence. The original media guru, Marshall McLuhan, once said that we don't know who first discovered water, but it probably wasn't the fish. And leading media influence activist Jean Kilbourne says ironically that young boys wearing Budweiser caps often tell her that the media don't influence them.Youth consistently underestimate the media's influence on them.

A May 2002 survey on teens, sex and TV shows that nearly three out of four (72%) teens think sex on TV influences the sexual behaviors of kids their age "somewhat" or "a lot"; but just one in four (22%) think it influences their own behavior.5 Influences are all the more powerful when we do not readily perceive them and cannot erect mental barriers against them.

Besides the pervasiveness of the media, there are neurological reasons that we do not perceive the influence of the media. Brain research demonstrates that we respond to images (the stock and trade of the mass communications media) differently than we respond to print. When we read books, we process the text in the neocortex (the higher cognitive thinking levels of the brain), and the process is slow and thoughtful. When we process images, we do it in the limbic system (a part of the brain so old that it is called the reptilian system), and the process is very rapid, through instinct, impulse, and emotion. This is the same part of the brain that produces the fight-or-flight response, which gets our adrenalin pumping without our conscious thought.

Critical thinking is essential to media literacy as a prevention strategy. The goal of media literacy in prevention is to move our responses to media images out of the limbic system and into the neocortex, where we can respond more thoughtfully and carefully to the messages the images are giving us. Media literacy allows youth to reflect on important life choices and make decisions about their health behaviors. It allows young people to control the influences of media messages, instead of being controlled by them.

Media literacy knowledge and skills are required to identify examples of product placement and understand the concept – that it is a kind of stealth advertising and that it has economic support and outcomes.

The goal of prevention in public health is to stop or moderate major human dysfunctions. Prevention efforts try to counteract the potential precursors of dysfunction, called risk factors, and reinforce the potential precursors of health, called protective factors. Risk factors are variables, such as poor school performance, that are associated with a high probability of developing risky behaviors. Protective factors refer to conditions, such as having media literacy skills, that improve people's resistance to risk factors.

Traditional prevention approaches, including social marketing through the media and intervention programs like Drug Abuse Resistance Education (DARE), focus on changing individual behavior. From this perspective, risk factors are in the individual. The obese person, for example, is viewed as lacking the willpower to say no to food and to exercise more frequently. The individual approach places most of its emphasis on providing education, knowledge, and skills to help people say no. Unfortunately, this approach has proved to be too simplistic and woefully inadequate.

This is evidenced by the fact that even though they receive lots of information from their schools and the media about the unhealthy consequences of tobacco use, 6,000 young people try a cigarette each day, and 3,000 go on to be regular smokers.

Today's prevention models keep traditional/ individual approaches in the prevention toolbox, but they emphasize the environmental, social, political, and cultural factors that encourage risky behavior and act as barriers to changing individual risky behavior. The media constitute just such a factor. Television, radio, movies, magazines, the Internet, videogames, billboards, and bumper stickers fill our environment with social, political, and cultural messages – some healthy and many unhealthy.

Successful prevention strategies must address the influence of the media, as well as attempt to change individual behavior. For example, while encouraging the potentially obese child to decrease energy intake and increase energy expenditure, we could also take some of the following actions, many of which are drawn from a much longer list recommended by Nestle and Jacobson.

— Restrict advertising of high-calorie, low-nutrient foods on television shows commonly watched by children, or require broadcasters to provide equal time for messages promoting healthy eating and physical activity.

— Require print advertisements to disclose the calorie content of the foods they are marketing.

— Eliminate the sale of soft drinks, candy bars, and foods high in calories, fat, or sugars in schools.

— Integrate media literacy throughout the comprehensive health curriculum standards in each state, as well as other appropriate curricular areas such as language arts and social studies.

— Require and fund daily physical education and sports programs in primary and secondary schools.

— Provide funding and other incentives for bicycle paths, recreation centers, swimming pools, safe parks, and sidewalks.

— Levy city, state, or federal taxes on soft drinks and other foods high in calories, fat, or sugar to fund a campaign for good nutrition and physical activity – the approach used in tobacco use prevention. We have a lot to learn in the science of prevention, but one thing we do know is that it is a complex subject

> requiring complex solutions. As a result, prevention is a difficult practice for many people, including legislators and policymakers, who are looking for a "quick fix" at the lowest cost.

Studying the long-term effects of teaching students media literacy skills is a complex and expensive task. We need much more research in the area of media literacy education and prevention. Some of the shortterm research and an abundance of anecdotal evidence from teachers, parents, media literacy professionals, and prevention specialists, however, suggest that media literacy works.

Media literacy helps children and adolescents gain skills to intelligently navigate the media and filter the hundreds of messages they receive every day. Simply put, media literacy is the ability to "ask questions about what you watch, see and read." Media literacy can help youth understand how media are developed, the approaches used to increase persuasion, the commercial sources and beneficiaries of advertising, and the ideology of messages contained in commercial and news media. When they recognize how media messages influence them, students can develop the skills they need to carefully reflect on the messages that portray risky lifestyle choices like smoking as glamorous, rebellious, or "cool."

Simply telling youth that they are influenced by the media doesn't work. They must have the chance to explore the concept under the guidance of teachers and parents who fully understand the concepts of media literacy and have the patience to allow youth to discover for themselves the extent to which they are influenced by the media. This process can be facilitated through a number of media literacy exercises that lead students through the process of personal discovery.

It is exasperating to see youngsters' eyes glaze over when someone tells them that they are influenced by the media and exciting to see the light come on in their eyes when they go through a co-learning process with a teacher/facilitator to discover the influence of media for themselves.

When youth learn to analyze the messages communicated by advertising, entertainment, and news media, they can uncover the values and points of view embedded in the messages and decide whether to accept or reject them. Learning to evaluate messages for accuracy, reliability, purpose, and bias gives students better information and tools with which to make decisions about their health risk behaviors. This is the focus of a number of comprehensive health curriculum standards in many states. In the short term, we believe that media knowledge and literacy skills will better enable youth to make healthy choices, even in the face of the barrage of unhealthy messages they receive from the media.

Media literacy is an essential life-skill for the 21st century . Here are some suggestions for fostering that skill in our young people.

— *You must be media literate to help children be media literate.* Teachers and parents must become media literate themselves so they can guide the development of media literacy in their students and children. Recognize that media literacy is a critical thinking life skill that requires significant learning and practice time to master. Even though the media may seem trivial sometimes, it is no trivial task to become media literate.

— *Familiarize yourself with youth media and culture.* Listen to their music, look at the websites they frequent, watch what they are watching on TV, and go to a teen movie once in a while. This will help you keep up with the rapidly changing world of youth media and culture and will give you credibility when you talk to kids about media and media literacy. You can also learn a lot about the media from youngsters.

— *Remember that media literacy is not media bashing.* Feel free to acknowledge your pleasure and that of youth in media use. Youth culture, especially, is closely identified with media and pop culture. Adults must validate and acknowledge young people's experiences and familiarity with their media culture before youth will accept and apply media literacy skills to the messages they consume daily.

— *Start media literacy as soon as children start watching TV.* Parents should start early with their children to experience media together and begin rudimentary analysis. Children are especially vulnerable to the impact of advertising. A recent study out of Stanford University found that one 30-second commercial can influence the brand choices of children as young as two years, and repeated exposures to ads are even more effective. Monitor your child's media consumption and engage in a continuing dialogue about the media messages. Ask them how an ad is different from a program and discuss the purpose of each. Talk to them about their favorite characters' actions and the real-life consequences of those actions, which are often not seen in the media. Help them distinguish between what is real and what is not.

— *Integrate media literacy skills in all curricular areas.* Language arts, social studies, and health are particularly appropriate, but media literacy skills have a place in history, geography, math, and science.

— *Get kids involved in media production.* Creating and producing their own media messages is a powerful strategy for helping youth internalize media literacy skills. This activity can be a "hook" to get them involved in media literacy and prevention programs. Put a video or still camera in their hands, give them an audio recorder, and teach them how to use software programs for creating graphics, animating, and editing. As they make media messages, guide them in the principles of media literacy that fit in with their experiences.

— *Give youth the power to make healthy decisions.* Not all kids are influenced by media messages in the same way. Nor are they passive dupes who are victimized by the media. Children bring different backgrounds to their experiences with the media, and they construct their own values and beliefs in active negotiation with these messages. Help them realize their power to accept healthy media messages, challenge unhealthy messages, and make good decisions for themselves.

Bibliography

Boone, Margaret S., "Practicing Sociomedicine: Redefining the Problem of Infant Mortality in Washington DC in Anthropological Praxis: Translating Knowledge into Action", Robert Wulff and Shirley Fiske, eds. Pp.56-71. Boulder, CO: Westview Press, 1987.

Cambridge, Vibert, "Second International Conference on Entertainment-Education", Email posting from 10/8/96, 1996.

Dennis, Everette E., "Of Media and People", Newbury Park, CA: SAGE Publications,1992.

Dunwoody, Sharon, and S.H. Stocking, "Social Scientists and Journalists: Confronting the Stereotypes in The Media", *Social Science and Social Policy for Children*, Eli Rubinstein and Jane Brown, eds. pp 167-185. Norwood, N.J.: Ablex Publishing, 1985

Felson, Richard B., "Mass Media Effects on Violent Behavior", *Annual Review of Sociology* 22:108-126, 1996.

Foster, Stanley O., J. Shepperd, J.H. Davis, and A.N. Agle, "Working With African Nations to Improve the Health of Their Children", *Journal of the American Medical Association* 263(24):3303-3305, 1990.

Garfinkel, Simson, "Children's Science Radio", *Technology Review* 96(7):18-19, 1993.

Gellert, George, K.V. Higgins, R.M. Lowery, and R.M. Maxwell 1994 A National Survey of Public Health Officers' Interactions with the Media. Journal of the American Medical Association 271(16):1285-1289.

Gundlach, James H., and Steven Stack, "The Impact of Hyper Media Coverage on Suicide":, New York City, 1910-1920. Social Science Quarterly 71(3):619-627, 1990.

Peroca, Norma, "Children and Television Advertising from a Social Science Perspective", *Critical Studies in Mass Communication* 12(3):354-64, 1996.

Rubinstein, Eli A. and Jane D. Brown, eds., "The Media, Social Science and Social Policy for Children", Norwood, NJ: Ablex Publishing, 1985

Index